Middle Ages, Renaissance, Reformation & Epistles

Second Edition

A Year of Lesson Plans
for History, Geography, and Bible
(Grades 1–12)

by Sonya Shafer

Middle Ages, Renaissance, Reformation & Epistles, Second Edition

Cover Design: John Shafer

ISBN 978-1-61634-371-2 printed
ISBN 978-1-61634-372-9 electronic download

Published by
Simply Charlotte Mason, LLC
930 New Hope Road #11-892
Lawrenceville, Georgia 30045
simplycharlottemason.com

Printed by PrintLogic, Inc.
Monroe, Georgia, USA

Contents

How to Use

This book of lesson plans contains book suggestions and assignments for every grade level, so you can combine all of your students into one family study.

- The **Family** instructions are for everyone to do together.
- **Additional Grade Level** assignments are given for students to complete either independently or with the parent. Your choice.

Complete one lesson per day to finish this study in a school year. The lesson plans in this book follow this five-day schedule.

Day 1	Day 2	Day 3	Day 4	Day 5
Family History *(plus Independent reading for grades 7–12)*	Grade Level History	Geography and Bible	Family History *(plus Independent reading for grades 7–12)*	Grade Level History

You will find lots of helpful information and Internet links on the Links and Tips page for this book at http://simplycm.com/middle-ages-links

Complete Year's Book List

Family (all students)

- *Around the World in a Hundred Years* by Jean Fritz
- Bible
- *The Bible Smuggler* by Louise Vernon
  Historical fiction that follows the story of William Tyndale.
- *Castle* by David Macaulay
- *A Castle with Many Rooms: The Story of the Middle Ages* by Lorene Lambert
- *Cathedral* by David Macaulay
- *Material World* **and** *Hungry Planet: What the World Eats* by Peter Menzel
  These two wonderful living geography books are used with our *Visits to . . .* books every year in all the grades.
- *The Stuff They Left Behind: From the Days of the Middle Ages* portfolio
  A collection of large full-color photographs of artifacts and architecture with leading thoughts and discussion questions.
- *Visits to South & Central America and Australia* notebook by Sonya Shafer (one for each student)
  Each *Visits to . . .* book guides your student to spend time exploring a continent or region through map work, living books, and the personal photographs and living travelogue contained in *Material World* and *Hungry Planet: What the World Eats.* Ideas are also included for additional activities.

plus . . .

Grades 1–3

- *Brother Francis and the Friendly Beasts* by Margaret Hodges
- *Castle Diary: The Journal of Tobias Burgess* by Richard Platt
- *Marguerite Makes a Book* by Bruce Robertson
- *Medieval Feast* by Aliki
- *Pippo the Fool* by Tracey E. Fern.
- *The Sword in the Tree* by Clyde Robert Bulla
- *Viking Adventure* by Clyde Robert Bulla

Grades 4–6

- *Adam of the Road* by Elizabeth Janet Gray
- *King Arthur and His Knights* audio recording by Jim Weiss
- "The Pied Piper of Hamelin" poem by Robert Browning
- *The Vikings* by Elizabeth Janeway

Grades 7–9

- Book of Centuries (one for each student)
- *Discovering Doctrine* by Sonya Shafer (one for each student)
  A multi-year project for observing, recording, and organizing Biblical truths as the student reads through the Bible.
- *In Freedom's Cause* by G. A. Henty
- *Life in the Word* by Sonya Shafer (one for each student)
  Students will learn different Bible study methods as they dig deeper into the same epistles covered in the Family Bible Study lessons outlined in this book.
- *The Magna Charta* by James Daugherty
- *The Prince and the Pauper* by Samuel Clemens (Mark Twain)

- *The Shining Company* by Rosemary Sutcliff
- *The Story of King Arthur and His Knights* by Howard Pyle
  A classic retelling in old English style. Students will be assigned only "The Book of Arthur" from this collection of stories.
- *The White Stag* by Kate Seredy
  Tells the story of Attila the Hun from the Huns' point of view. The actual battles and violence are downplayed in favor of giving the big picture. Almost a fairy tale-style. Good discussion starter, especially the parts that include their religious beliefs.

Grades 10–12

- *The Black Arrow* by Robert Louis Stevenson
- Book of Centuries (one for each student)
- *Discovering Doctrine* by Sonya Shafer (one for each student)
  A multi-year project for observing, recording, and organizing Biblical truths as the student reads through the Bible.
- *Famous Men of the Middle Ages,* with extra chapters by Rob Shearer (2008 edition, published by Greenleaf Press)
- *Famous Men of the Renaissance and Reformation* by Rob Shearer
- *The King's Fifth* by Scott O'Dell
- *The Lantern Bearers* by Rosemary Sutcliff
- *Life in the Word* by Sonya Shafer (one for each student)
  Students will learn different Bible study methods as they dig deeper into the same epistles covered in the Family Bible Study lessons outlined in this book.
- *Men of Iron* by Howard Pyle
- *The Second Mrs. Giaconda* by E. L. Konigsburg
- *Voices of the Renaissance and Reformation,* edited by Rob Shearer
  A collection of original source documents from the time period.

Other Materials

- 6 envelopes; paper
- Hammer or picture of a hammer
- Map of Paul's Journeys
- Small white board; dry-erase markers
- (optional) Various resources for hands-on projects

Suggestions for
Where to Find the Books

Simply Charlotte Mason

- Book of Centuries (one for each student in grades 7–12)
- *A Castle with Many Rooms: The Story of the Middle Ages* by Lorene Lambert (Family)
- *Discovering Doctrine* by Sonya Shafer (one for each student in grades 7–12)
- *Life in the Word* by Sonya Shafer (one for each student in grades 7–12)
- *The Magna Charta* by James Daugherty (grades 7–9)
- *Material World* **and** *Hungry Planet: What the World Eats* by Peter Menzel (Family)
- *The Stuff They Left Behind: From the Days of the Middle Ages* portfolio (Family)
- *The Vikings* by Elizabeth Janeway (grades 4–6)
- *Visits to South & Central America and Australia* notebook by Sonya Shafer (one for each student)

Public Domain

(You can probably download these for free at http://gutenberg.org, http://books.google.com, or http://archive.org.)

- *The Black Arrow* by Robert Louis Stevenson (grades 10–12)
- *In Freedom's Cause* by G. A. Henty (grades 7–9)
- *Men of Iron* by Howard Pyle (grades 10–12)
- "The Pied Piper of Hamelin" poem by Robert Browning (grades 4–6)
- *The Prince and the Pauper* by Samuel Clemens (Mark Twain) (grades 7–9)
- *The Story of King Arthur and His Knights* by Howard Pyle (grades 7–9 are assigned only "The Book of Arthur" in this collection of stories)

Your Local Library

(These are the titles that a library is most likely to have. You might also check for the titles listed under Your Favorite Book Store. If your library does not have access to a book listed here, add it to your Book Store list.)

- *Adam of the Road* by Elizabeth Janet Gray (grades 4–6)
- *Brother Francis and the Friendly Beasts* by Margaret Hodges (grades 1–3)
- *Castle* by David Macaulay (Family)
- *Castle Diary: The Journal of Tobias Burgess* by Richard Platt (grades 1–3)
- *Cathedral* by David Macaulay (Family)
- *The King's Fifth* by Scott O'Dell (grades 10–12)
- *Marguerite Makes a Book* by Bruce Robertson (grades 1–3)
- *Medieval Feast* by Aliki (grades 1–3)
- *Pippo the Fool* by Tracey E. Fern (grades 1–3)
- *The Sword in the Tree* by Clyde Robert Bulla (grades 1–3)
- *Viking Adventure* by Clyde Robert Bulla (grades 1–3)

Your Favorite Book Store

(Check http://amazon.com, http://christianbook.com, http://rainbowresource.com, or other favorite book sources.)

- *Around the World in a Hundred Years* by Jean Fritz (Family)
- *The Bible Smuggler* by Louise Vernon (Family)
- *Famous Men of the Middle Ages,* with extra chapters by Rob Shearer (2008 edition, published by Greenleaf Press) (grades 10–12)
- *Famous Men of the Renaissance and Reformation* by Rob Shearer (grades 10–12)

- *King Arthur and His Knights* audio recording by Jim Weiss (grades 4–6)
- *The Lantern Bearers* by Rosemary Sutcliff (grades 10–12)
- *The Second Mrs. Giaconda* by E. L. Konigsburg (grades 10–12)
- *The Shining Company* by Rosemary Sutcliff (grades 7–9)
- *Voices of the Renaissance and Reformation,* edited by Rob Shearer (grades 10–12)
- *The White Stag* by Kate Seredy (grades 7–9)

Visit http://simplycm.com/middle-ages-links for helpful links to the books.

Term 1

(12 weeks; 5 lessons/week)

Term 1 Book List

Family

- Bible
- *Castle* by David Macaulay
- *A Castle with Many Rooms: The Story of the Middle Ages* by Lorene Lambert
- *Material World* **and** *Hungry Planet: What the World Eats* by Peter Menzel
- *The Stuff They Left Behind: From the Days of the Middle Ages* portfolio
- *Visits to South & Central America and Australia* notebook by Sonya Shafer (one for each student)

Plus . . .

Grades 1–3

- *Viking Adventure* by Clyde Robert Bulla

Grades 4–6

- *The Vikings* by Elizabeth Janeway

Grades 7–9

- Book of Centuries (one for each student)
- *Discovering Doctrine* by Sonya Shafer (one for each student)
- *Life in the Word* by Sonya Shafer (one for each student)
- *The Shining Company* by Rosemary Sutcliff
- *The Story of King Arthur and His Knights* by Howard Pyle
- *The White Stag* by Kate Seredy

Grades 10–12

- Book of Centuries (one for each student)
- *Discovering Doctrine* by Sonya Shafer (one for each student)
- *Famous Men of the Middle Ages,* with extra chapters by Rob Shearer (2008 edition, published by Greenleaf Press)
- *The Lantern Bearers* by Rosemary Sutcliff
- *Life in the Word* by Sonya Shafer (one for each student)
- *Men of Iron* by Howard Pyle

What You Will Cover As a Family

History: *From the fall of Rome through the Crusades (376–1200)*

Geography: *Medieval Europe; Australia and Oceania*

Bible: *James and Galatians*

Term 1 At a Glance

	Family	Grades 1–3	Grades 4–6	Grades 7–9	Grades 10–12
Week 1, Lessons 1–5					
History	A Castle with Many Rooms, ch. 1, 2	Viking Adventure, ch. 1, 2	The Vikings, ch. 1	The White Stag, parts 1–4A	Famous Men of the Middle Ages, ch. 1, 2; The Lantern Bearers, ch. 1–4
Geography	Visits to South and Central America, Australia, Visit 1				
Bible	James 1			Life in the Word, ch. 1, lesson 1	Life in the Word, ch. 1, lesson 1
Week 2, Lessons 6–10					
History	A Castle with Many Rooms, ch. 3, 4	Viking Adventure, ch. 3, 4	The Vikings, ch. 2	The White Stag, part 4B; Story of King Arthur, Prologue, Book 1, ch. 1	Famous Men of the Middle Ages, ch. 3, 4; The Lantern Bearers, ch. 5–8
Geography	Visits to South and Central America, Australia, Visit 2				
Bible	James 2			Life in the Word, ch. 1, lesson 2	Life in the Word, ch. 1, lesson 2
Week 3, Lessons 11–15					
History	A Castle with Many Rooms, ch. 5, 6	Viking Adventure, ch. 5, 6	The Vikings, ch. 3	Story of King Arthur, Book I, ch. 2, 3; Book II, ch. 1, 2	Famous Men of the Middle Ages, ch. 5, 6; The Lantern Bearers, ch. 9–12
Geography	Visits to South and Central America, Australia, Visit 3				
Bible	James 3			Life in the Word, ch. 1, lesson 3	Life in the Word, ch. 1, lesson 3
Week 4, Lessons 16–20					
History	A Castle with Many Rooms, ch. 7, 8	Viking Adventure, ch. 7, 8	The Vikings, ch. 4	Story of King Arthur, Book II, ch. 3; Book III, ch. 1, 2	Famous Men of the Middle Ages, ch. 7, 8; The Lantern Bearers, ch. 13–16
Geography	Visits to South and Central America, Australia, Visit 4				
Bible	James 4			Life in the Word, ch. 1, lesson 4	Life in the Word, ch. 1, lesson 4
Week 5, Lessons 21–25					
History	A Castle with Many Rooms, ch. 9, 10	Viking Adventure, ch. 9, 10	The Vikings, ch. 5	Story of King Arthur, Book III, ch. 3–6	Famous Men of the Middle Ages, ch. 9, 10; The Lantern Bearers, ch. 17–20
Geography	Visits to South and Central America, Australia, Visit 5				
Bible	James 5			Life in the Word, ch. 1, lesson 5	Life in the Word, ch. 1, lesson 5
Week 6, Lessons 26–30					
History	A Castle with Many Rooms, ch. 11, 12	Viking Adventure, ch. 11, 12	The Vikings, ch. 6	The Shining Company, ch. 1–3	Famous Men of the Middle Ages, ch. 11, 12; The Lantern Bearers, ch. 21, 22; Men of Iron, ch. 1, 2
Geography	Visits to South and Central America, Australia, Visit 6				
Bible	Galatians 1			Life in the Word, ch. 2, lesson 1	Life in the Word, ch. 2, lesson 1

Use this chart to see what your family and each of your students will be studying week by week during this term. You will also be able to see when each book is scheduled to be used.

	Family	Grades 1-3	Grades 4-6	Grades 7-9	Grades 10-12
			Week 7, Lessons 31-35		
History	A Castle with Many Rooms, ch. 13, 14	Viking Adventure, ch. 13, 14	The Vikings, ch. 7	The Shining Company, ch. 4-7	Famous Men of the Middle Ages, ch. 13, 14; Men of Iron, ch. 3-10
Geography	Visits to South and Central America, Australia, Visit 7				
Bible	Galatians 2			Life in the Word, ch. 2, lesson 2	Life in the Word, ch. 2, lesson 2
			Week 8, Lessons 36-40		
History	A Castle with Many Rooms, ch. 15, 16	Viking Adventure, ch. 15, 16	The Vikings, ch. 8	The Shining Company, ch. 8-10	Famous Men of the Middle Ages, ch. 15, 16; Men of Iron, ch. 11-17
Geography	Visits to South and Central America, Australia, Visit 8				
Bible	Galatians 3			Life in the Word, ch. 3, lesson 1	Life in the Word, ch. 3, lesson 1
			Week 9, Lessons 41-45		
History	A Castle with Many Rooms, ch. 17, 18	Viking Adventure, ch. 17, 18	The Vikings, ch. 9	The Shining Company, ch. 11-14	Famous Men of the Middle Ages, ch. 17, 18; Men of Iron, ch. 18-22
Geography	Visits to South and Central America, Australia, Visit 9				
Bible	Galatians 4			Life in the Word, ch. 3, lesson 2	Life in the Word, ch. 3, lesson 2
			Week 10, Lessons 46-50		
History	Castle, parts 1, 2	Viking Adventure, ch. 19, 20	The Vikings, ch. 10	The Shining Company, ch. 15-18	Famous Men of the Middle Ages, ch. 19, 20; Men of Iron, ch. 23-28
Geography	Visits to South and Central America, Australia, Visit 10				
Bible	Galatians 5			Life in the Word, ch. 3, lesson 3	Life in the Word, ch. 3, lesson 3
			Week 11, Lessons 51-55		
History	Castle, parts 3, 4	Viking Adventure, ch. 21	The Vikings, ch. 11	The Shining Company, ch. 19-21	Famous Men of the Middle Ages, ch. 21, 22; Men of Iron, ch. 29-Conclusion
Geography	Visits to South and Central America, Australia, Visit 11				
Bible	Galatians 6			Life in the Word, ch. 4	Life in the Word, ch. 4
			Week 12, Lessons 56-60		
History	Exams or Catch Up or Project				
Geography	Visits to South and Central America, Australia, Visit 12				
Bible	Exams or Catch Up				

Lesson 1: The Long Fall of Rome

Materials Needed

- *A Castle with Many Rooms: The Story of the Middle Ages*
- *The White Stag* (grades 7–9)
- *The Lantern Bearers* (grades 10–12)

Family: Read together *A Castle with Many Rooms: The Story of the Middle Ages,* chapter 1, "The Long Fall," using the map on page 273, The Roman Empire in the 4th Century, to locate the Danube River. Ask for an oral narration.

Tip: *For younger children, you may want to break up the reading into two or more shorter sections and ask for a narration for each section. You could alternately read part of the chapter today and the rest tomorrow.*

Grades 7–9: Read together or assign as independent reading *The White Stag,* part I, "Nimrod, the Mighty Hunter."

Grades 10–12: Assign as independent reading *The Lantern Bearers,* chapter 1, "The Terrace Steps."

Book of Centuries Timeline

Alaric the Visigoth sacks Rome (410)

Attila the Hun invades the Roman Empire (434–453)

Vandals sack Rome (455)

End of the Western Roman Empire (476)

Lesson 2: Various History Readings

Materials Needed

- *Viking Adventure* (grades 1–3)
- *The Vikings* (grades 4–6)
- *The White Stag* (grades 7–9)
- *Famous Men of the Middle Ages* (grades 10–12)
- *The Lantern Bearers* (grades 10–12)

Grades 1–3: Read together *Viking Adventure*, chapter 1, "Olaf the Strong."

Grades 4–6: Read together or assign as independent reading *The Vikings,* the first half of chapter 1, "Outlawed!"

Grades 7–9: Read together or assign as independent reading *The White Stag,* part II, "Twin Eagles of Hadur."

Grades 10–12: Read together or assign as independent reading *Famous Men of the Middle Ages,* chapter 1, "Alaric the Visigoth," and ask for a written narration. Also assign as independent reading, *The Lantern Bearers,* chapter 2, "Rutupiae Light."

Tip: *Encourage your high school student not to read both assignments back to back. He will find it easier to pay full attention and to retain*

Book of Centuries Timeline

what he is reading if he separates the two books, doing them at different times of the day.

Lesson 3: Visit 1 to Australia & James 1

Materials Needed

- *Visits to South & Central America and Australia*
- Bible
- Envelope; 2 sheets of paper
- *Life in the Word* (grades 7–12)

Family Geography: Complete visit 1 in *Visits to South & Central America and Australia.*

Family Bible Study: Write *epistle* on a small white board or sheet of paper. Show students the word and explain that *epistle* means "letter." During the time of the early church, the followers of Jesus would write letters to encourage and instruct each other. This year you are going to look at several epistles of the early church. You will discover what was going on when each letter was written and see what you can learn from them.

Jesus raised from the dead (30)

James believes in Jesus (30)

James writes his letter to scattered Jewish believers (c. 40–45)

Explain that some epistles are named after the person who wrote them and some are named after the people who received them. The first epistle you will look at is called "James," for it was written by James, the half-brother of Jesus. He wrote it to encourage a group of Jews who had been run out of their homes because they believed in Jesus and had fled to other towns and countries. These refugees were facing many tough situations, or trials, of various kinds as they scattered and tried to find another place to live and work.

Have students address an envelope that reflects the epistle of James: put who it was from in the return address area and to whom it was written in the middle front. Label one sheet of paper "What To Do" and another paper "What Not To Do."

Read together James 1, a paragraph at a time. Ask students to listen especially for James' counsel about What To Do in a trial, or tough situation, and What Not To Do. Pause after each paragraph and ask students to share what they discovered: verses 1–4, 5–8, 9–11, 12–15, 16–18, 19–21, 22–25, 26–27. (Example: Count it as joy; Ask God for wisdom; Don't waver or doubt; etc.). Record their discoveries on the appropriate papers. Fold the papers and keep them in the envelope; you will add to them as you study each chapter of James in the coming weeks.

***Tip:** The easiest way to record their suggestions would be in words, but be open to other possibilities that might help students grasp the ideas in these passages. For example, you could draw sketches, or allow the students to draw their own sketches, and caption each one.*

Focus on James 1:19–21. Discuss: What can we learn from these verses about what to do or not to do when we are in tough situations? What do we usually tend to do when we're in a trial? Why might it be especially important to be quick to listen, slow to speak, and slow to anger when we are in a tough situation?

***Tip:** If an entire chapter would be too much for your students, feel free to spread out the lesson over several days, covering one paragraph per day, or to read and discuss only the "Focus on" verses.*

Grades 7–12: Help students to complete or assign as independent work *Life in the Word,* chapter 1, "Book Study of James," lesson 1.

Older students should be working on the long-term project of *Discovering Doctrine*. As they read through Scripture for schoolwork, in personal Bible study, or when listening to sermons, they should be looking and listening for any doctrinal truths about the ten major doctrines listed in the notebook: Bible, God the Father, Jesus Christ, Holy Spirit, angels, man, sin, salvation, the church, future events. Whenever they discover a doctrinal truth in Scripture, they should record it in the appropriate section of *Discovering Doctrine* along with the Bible reference where they found it.

***Tip:** After they have read through the entire Bible (over several years) and recorded the doctrinal truths they have found there, they may summarize each section and compose a personal doctrinal statement.*

Lesson 4: Justinian the Great

Materials Needed

- *A Castle with Many Rooms: The Story of the Middle Ages*
- *The White Stag* (grades 7–9)
- *The Lantern Bearers* (grades 10–12)

Family: Ask students what they recall from last time's reading about the Fall of the Roman Empire. Explain that in today's reading they will hear about one ruler who hoped to reclaim the empire. Write the names "Constantinople (Byzantium)" and "Justinian" on a small white board or sheet of paper for students to see. Read together *A Castle with Many Rooms: The Story of the Middle Ages,* chapter 2, "Justinian the Great." Help students find Constantinople on the map on page 274, Europe in the Time of Odoacer, when it is mentioned in the chapter. Ask for an oral narration.

***Tip:** Narrations can be done in many ways. You may want to assign older children to do written narrations. Or visit our website at* http://simplycm.com/narration-ideas *for many more creative ideas that encourage students to narrate.*

Book of Centuries Timeline

Justinian codifies Roman laws (534) and builds the Hagia Sophia (537)

Book of Centuries Timeline

Grades 7–9: Read together or assign as independent reading *The White Stag,* part III, "White Eagle of the Moon."

Grades 10–12: Assign as independent reading *The Lantern Bearers,* chapter 3, "The Wolves of the Sea."

***Reminder:** Get* The Story of King Arthur and His Knights *for lesson 9 for grades 7–9.*

Lesson 5: Various History Readings

Materials Needed

- *Viking Adventure* (grades 1–3)
- *The Vikings* (grades 4–6)
- *The White Stag* (grades 7–9)
- *Famous Men of the Middle Ages* (grades 10–12)
- *The Lantern Bearers* (grades 10–12)

Grades 1–3: Read together *Viking Adventure,* chapter 2, "The Feast."

Grades 4–6: Read together or assign as independent reading *The Vikings,* the last half of chapter 1, "Outlawed!"

Grades 7–9: Read together or assign as independent reading *The White Stag,* the first half of part IV, "Attila."

Augustine serves as Bishop of Hippo Regius in Roman Africa, writes The City of God and Confessions (354–430)

Grades 10–12: Read together or assign as independent reading *Famous Men of the Middle Ages,* chapter 2, "Augustine of Hippo," and ask for a written narration. Also assign as independent reading, *The Lantern Bearers,* chapter 4, "Ullasfjord."

***Tip:** Make sure older children are up to date with their* Discovering Doctrine *notebooks and their Book of Centuries entries.*

Lesson 6: King Arthur and the Saxons

Materials Needed

- *A Castle with Many Rooms: The Story of the Middle Ages*
- *The White Stag* (grades 7–9)
- *The Lantern Bearers* (grades 10–12)

King Arthur defends Britain from the Saxons (485)

Saxons conquer Britain (600)

Family: Ask students what they recall from last time's reading about Justinian and Constantinople. Explain that they will now hear about what was happening in another part of the Roman Empire while the Goths were advancing on Rome. Read together *A Castle with Many Rooms: The Story of the Middle Ages,* chapter 3, "King Arthur and the Saxons," and ask for an oral narration. Use the maps on pages 274 and 275 to help students see what they are reading about.

Grades 7–9: Read together or assign as independent reading *The White Stag,* the last half of part IV, "Attila."

Grades 10–12: Assign as independent reading *The Lantern Bearers,* chapter 5, "Wild Geese Flighting."

Book of Centuries Timeline

 Lesson 7: Various History Readings

Materials Needed
- *Viking Adventure* (grades 1–3)
- *The Vikings* (grades 4–6)
- *The White Stag*, if needed (grades 7–9)
- *Famous Men of the Middle Ages* (grades 10–12)
- *The Lantern Bearers* (grades 10–12)

Grades 1–3: Read together *Viking Adventure,* chapter 3, "The Land Across the Sea."

Grades 4–6: Read together or assign as independent reading *The Vikings,* the first half of chapter 2, "Land to the West."

Grades 7–9: Use today to catch up and finish reading *The White Stag* if needed.

Grades 10–12: Read together or assign as independent reading *Famous Men of the Middle Ages,* chapter 3, "Gaiseric the Vandal," and ask for a written narration. Also assign as independent reading, *The Lantern Bearers,* chapter 6, "The Saxon Wind."

Gaiseric the Vandal sacks Rome (427–477)

 Lesson 8: Visit 2 to Australia & James 2

Materials Needed
- *Visits to South & Central America and Australia*
- Bible
- James envelope and papers
- *Life in the Word* (grades 7–12)

Family Geography: Complete visit 2 in *Visits to South & Central America and Australia.*

Family Bible Study: Ask students what they recall about the epistle of

Book of Centuries Timeline

James from last time's introduction and reading of chapter 1 (or 1:19–21). Allow them to look at the James envelope and the papers they started last time to prompt review. Explain that another thing it's easy to start doing when you're in a trial is to pick and choose who you're going to be nice to based on whether you think that person can help you. James brought up that topic next.

Read together James 2, a paragraph at a time. Ask students to listen for more of James' counsel about What To Do in a trial and What Not To Do in a tough situation. Pause after each paragraph and ask students to share what they discovered: verses 1–7, 8–13, 14–17, 18–26. Record students' suggestions on your ongoing papers.

Focus on James 2:1–9. Discuss: What can we learn from these verses about what to do or not to do when we are in tough situations? What does *partiality* mean? Is this passage saying that we should not respect some people more than others? Why? What is the difference between showing partiality and showing respect?

Tip: *If an entire chapter would be too much for your students, feel free to spread out the lesson over several days, covering one paragraph per day, or to read and discuss only the "Focus on" verses.*

Grades 7–12: Help students to complete or assign as independent work *Life in the Word,* chapter 1, "Book Study of James," lesson 2.

Lesson 9: The Monastery

Materials Needed

- *A Castle with Many Rooms: The Story of the Middle Ages*
- *The Stuff They Left Behind: From the Days of the Middle Ages*
- *The Story of King Arthur and His Knights* (grades 7–9)
- *The Lantern Bearers* (grades 10–12)

Benedict writes the rules for monks (529)

Family: Ask students what they recall from last time's reading about Britain and the Saxons. On the map on page 276 of *A Castle with Many Rooms,* England after the English Conquest, help students locate Lindisfarne off the northeast coast of Britain. Display and discuss the picture of the Lindisfarne Gospels in *The Stuff They Left Behind: From the Days of the Middle Ages.* Write the word "monastery" on a small white board or sheet of paper and explain that students will find out more about the Lindisfarne monastery and other monasteries in today's reading. Read together *A Castle with Many Rooms: The Story of the Middle Ages,* chapter 4, "The Monastery," and ask for an oral narration.

Grades 7–9: Read together or assign as independent reading *The Story of King Arthur and His Knights,* "The Book of King Arthur," Prologue.

Grades 10–12: Assign as independent reading *The Lantern Bearers,* chapter 7, "The Woman in the Doorway."

 Lesson 10: Various History Readings

Materials Needed

- *Viking Adventure* (grades 1–3)
- *The Vikings* (grades 4–6)
- *The Story of King Arthur and His Knights* (grades 7–9)
- *Famous Men of the Middle Ages* (grades 10–12)
- *The Lantern Bearers* (grades 10–12)

Grades 1–3: Read together *Viking Adventure,* chapter 4, "Rolf."

Grades 4–6: Read together or assign as independent reading *The Vikings,* the last half of chapter 2, "Land to the West."

Grades 7–9: Read together or assign as independent reading *The Story of King Arthur and His Knights,* "The Book of King Arthur," part I, chapter 1.

Grades 10–12: Read together or assign as independent reading *Famous Men of the Middle Ages,* chapter 4, "Patrick of Ireland," and ask for a written narration. Also assign as independent reading, *The Lantern Bearers,* chapter 8, "Singing Magic."

***Tip:** Make sure older children are up to date with their* Discovering Doctrine *notebooks and their Book of Centuries entries.*

Book of Centuries Timeline

Patrick captured by Irish slavers; escapes and becomes missionary to Ireland (432)

 Lesson 11: The Earliest Explorers

Materials Needed

- *A Castle with Many Rooms: The Story of the Middle Ages*
- *The Story of King Arthur and His Knights* (grades 7–9)
- *The Lantern Bearers* (grades 10–12)

Family: Ask students what they recall from last time's reading about monasteries. Explain that while some monks were content to stay at their monasteries, others were eager to explore the unknown world. Write "Brendan the Navigator" on a small white board or sheet of paper. Read together *A Castle with Many Rooms: The Story of the Middle Ages,* chapter 5, "The Earliest Explorers," using the world map on page 284 to track these explorers' journeys. Add the name "Leif" to the white board when you come to his story in the chapter. Ask for an oral narration.

Brendan the Navigator, who explored the Atlantic (484–577)

First Viking colonies established in Greenland by Erik the Red (982)

Grades 7–9: Read together or assign as independent reading *The Story of King Arthur and His Knights,* "The Book of King Arthur," part I, chapter 2.

Grades 10–12: Assign as independent reading *The Lantern Bearers,* chapter 9, "Forest Sanctuary."

Book of Centuries Timeline

Lesson 12: Various History Readings

Materials Needed

- *Viking Adventure* (grades 1–3)
- *The Vikings* (grades 4–6)
- *The Story of King Arthur and His Knights* (grades 7–9)
- *Famous Men of the Middle Ages* (grades 10–12)
- *The Lantern Bearers* (grades 10–12)

Grades 1–3: Read together *Viking Adventure,* chapter 5, "Old Bard."

Grades 4–6: Read together or assign as independent reading *The Vikings,* the first half of chapter 3, "The Voyage to Greenland."

Grades 7–9: Read together or assign as independent reading *The Story of King Arthur and His Knights,* "The Book of King Arthur," part I, chapter 3.

Attila the Hun invades the Roman Empire (434–453)

Grades 10–12: Read together or assign as independent reading *Famous Men of the Middle Ages,* chapter 5, "Attila the Hun," and ask for a written narration. Also assign as independent reading, *The Lantern Bearers,* chapter 10, "The Fortress of the High Powers."

Lesson 13: Visit 3 to Australia & James 3

Materials Needed

- *Visits to South & Central America and Australia*
- *Hungry Planet: What the World Eats*
- Bible
- James envelope and papers
- *Life in the Word* (grades 7–12)

Family Geography: Complete visit 3 in *Visits to South & Central America and Australia.*

Family Bible Study: Ask students what they recall about the epistle of James so far. Allow them to look at the James envelope and papers they have created to prompt review. Explain that when we are in the middle of a trial, we can receive advice from many different people, people seeking to teach us what they think we should do. How will we know whose words to follow and whose to ignore? James gave his readers some guidelines.

Read together James 3, a paragraph at a time. Ask students to listen for more of James' counsel about What To Do in a trial and What Not To Do in a tough situation. Pause after each paragraph and ask students to share what they discovered: verses 1–5, 6–12, 13–18. Record students' suggestions on your ongoing papers.

Focus on James 3:13–18. Discuss: Describe (and define as needed) the characteristics of godly wisdom. How can we use those characteristics to help us decide what would be the wisest thing to do when we are in a tough situation?

Grades 7–12: Help students to complete or assign as independent work *Life in the Word,* chapter 1, "Book Study of James," lesson 3.

Book of Centuries Timeline

Lesson 14: Making a Nation

Materials Needed

- *A Castle with Many Rooms: The Story of the Middle Ages*
- *The Story of King Arthur and His Knights* (grades 7–9)
- *The Lantern Bearers* (grades 10–12)

Family: Ask students what they recall from last time's reading about early explorers, Brendan the Navigator and Erik the Red and his son Leif. Explain that when Brendan was a young boy, thinking about conquering the sea, another young boy was setting his sights on conquering more land. Write the name "Clovis" on a small white board or sheet of paper. Read together *A Castle with Many Rooms: The Story of the Middle Ages,* chapter 6, "Making a Nation," using the map on page 274, Europe in the Time of Odoacer, to help students find the kingdom of the Franks. Ask for an oral narration.

Clovis unites the Franks into a nation in Gaul (481–511)

Grades 7–9: Read together or assign as independent reading *The Story of King Arthur and His Knights,* "The Book of King Arthur," part II, chapter 1.

Grades 10–12: Assign as independent reading *The Lantern Bearers,* chapter 11, "The Young Foxes."

Lesson 15: Various History Readings

Materials Needed

- *Viking Adventure* (grades 1–3)
- *The Vikings* (grades 4–6)
- *The Story of King Arthur and His Knights* (grades 7–9)
- *Famous Men of the Middle Ages* (grades 10–12)
- *The Lantern Bearers* (grades 10–12)

Grades 1–3: Read together *Viking Adventure,* chapter 6, "Tales Before the Fire."

Grades 4–6: Read together or assign as independent reading *The Vikings,* the last half of chapter 3, "The Voyage to Greenland."

Grades 7–9: Read together or assign as independent reading *The Story of King Arthur and His Knights,* "The Book of King Arthur," part II, chapter 2.

Grades 10–12: Read together or assign as independent reading *Famous Men of the Middle Ages,* chapter 6, "Theodoric the Ostrogoth," and ask for a

Theodoric the Ostrogoth rules Italy (475–526)

Book of Centuries Timeline

written narration. Also assign as independent reading, *The Lantern Bearers,* chapter 12, "Brown Sister, Golden Sister."

Tip: Make sure older children are up to date with their Discovering Doctrine *notebooks and their Book of Centuries entries.*

 Lesson 16: The Scroll and the Stone

Materials Needed

- *A Castle with Many Rooms: The Story of the Middle Ages*
- *The Story of King Arthur and His Knights* (grades 7–9)
- *The Lantern Bearers* (grades 10–12)

Family: Ask students what they recall from last time's reading about Clovis and the Franks. Look at the map on page 274 of *A Castle with Many Rooms,* Europe in the Time of Odoacer, and do a brief review of what has been learned so far. Point to each of the following locations in turn and ask students if they remember what was happening there during the Middle Ages: Ireland (Brendan the Navigator explored to the west); Scandinavia (Erik and Leif explored Iceland, Greenland, and Newfoundland); Britain (Saxons invaded); Kingdom of the Franks (expanded into Gaul); Rome (no longer ruled); Constantinople (Justinian compiled the Roman law). Explain that in today's reading they will hear about what was happening farther east. Read together *A Castle with Many Rooms: The Story of the Middle Ages,* chapter 7, "The Scroll and the Stone," and ask for an oral narration.

Muhammad founds the religion of Islam (570–632)

Grades 7–9: Read together or assign as independent reading *The Story of King Arthur and His Knights,* "The Book of King Arthur," part II, the first half of chapter 3.

Grades 10–12: Assign as independent reading *The Lantern Bearers,* chapter 13, "The Empty Hut."

 Lesson 17: Various History Readings

Materials Needed

- *Viking Adventure* (grades 1–3)
- *The Vikings* (grades 4–6)
- *The Story of King Arthur and His Knights* (grades 7–9)
- *Famous Men of the Middle Ages* (grades 10–12)
- *The Lantern Bearers* (grades 10–12)

Grades 1–3: Read together *Viking Adventure,* chapter 7, "The Horseman."

Grades 4–6: Read together or assign as independent reading *The Vikings,* the first half of chapter 4, "A New Home—and a New Land."

Grades 7–9: Read together or assign as independent reading *The Story of King Arthur and His Knights,* "The Book of King Arthur," part II, the last half of chapter 3.

Grades 10–12: Read together or assign as independent reading *Famous Men of the Middle Ages,* chapter 7, "Clovis," and ask for a written narration. Also assign as independent reading, *The Lantern Bearers,* chapter 14, "The Honour of First Blood."

***Reminder:** Get* The Shining Company *for lesson 27 for grades 7–9.*

Lesson 18: Visit 4 to Australia & James 4

Materials Needed

- *Visits to South & Central America and Australia*
- Bible
- James envelope and papers
- *Life in the Word* (grades 7–12)

Family Geography: Complete visit 4 in *Visits to South & Central America and Australia.*

Family Bible Study: Ask students what they recall about the epistle of James from chapters 1–3. Allow students to look at the James envelope and papers they have created to prompt review. Explain that fights and quarrels were breaking out among the believers James wrote to. James wanted them to understand that we all have things we want; those desires are not necessarily bad. But when we become proud and think that our desires are all that matter—that they are more important than anyone else's desires or even more important than what God wants us to do—that's what causes fights.

Read together James 4, a paragraph at a time. Ask students to listen for more of James' counsel about What To Do and What Not To Do in a tough situation. Pause after each paragraph and ask students to share what they discovered: verses 1–10, 11–12, 13–17. Record students' suggestions on your ongoing papers.

Focus on James 4:1–10. Discuss: Why is it especially easy to fight or quarrel when we are in the midst of a trial? How can we avoid quarrels? What does it mean to humble yourself?

***Tip:** Remember, if an entire chapter would be too much for your students, feel free to spread out the lesson over several days, covering one paragraph per day, or to read and discuss only the "Focus on" verses.*

Book of Centuries Timeline

Book of Centuries Timeline

Grades 7–12: Help students to complete or assign as independent work *Life in the Word,* chapter 1, "Book Study of James," lesson 4.

 Lesson 19: Charles the Hammer

Materials Needed

- *A Castle with Many Rooms: The Story of the Middle Ages*
- A hammer or a picture of a hammer
- *The Story of King Arthur and His Knights* (grades 7–9)
- *The Lantern Bearers* (grades 10–12)

Charles the Hammer defeats the Muslims, halts their westward expansion (714–741)

Family: Ask students what they recall from last time's reading about Mohammed and the Muslims. Read again the final statements from chapter 7: "It seemed that none would stand before them. But one would and did." Show students a hammer or a picture of a hammer and explain that in today's reading they will meet the one who stood before the Muslim army and find out what a hammer has to do with the story. Read together *A Castle with Many Rooms: The Story of the Middle Ages,* chapter 8, "Charles the Hammer," using the map on page 274, Europe in the Time of Odoacer, to help students follow the story. Ask for an oral narration.

Grades 7–9: Read together or assign as independent reading *The Story of King Arthur and His Knights,* "The Book of King Arthur," part III, chapter 1.

Grades 10–12: Assign as independent reading *The Lantern Bearers,* chapter 15, "The Hawking Glove."

 Lesson 20: Various History Readings

Materials Needed

- *Viking Adventure* (grades 1–3)
- *The Vikings* (grades 4–6)
- *The Story of King Arthur and His Knights* (grades 7–9)
- *Famous Men of the Middle Ages* (grades 10–12)
- *The Lantern Bearers* (grades 10–12)

Grades 1–3: Read together *Viking Adventure,* chapter 8, "Olaf's Answer."

Grades 4–6: Read together or assign as independent reading *The Vikings,* the last half of chapter 4, "A New Home—and a New Land."

Grades 7–9: Read together or assign as independent reading *The Story of King Arthur and His Knights,* "The Book of King Arthur," part III, chapter 2.

Grades 10–12: Read together or assign as independent reading *Famous Men of the Middle Ages,* chapter 8, "Justinian the Great," and ask for a written narration. Also assign as independent reading, *The Lantern Bearers,* chapter 16, "White Thorn and Yellow Iris."

***Tip:** Make sure older children are up to date with their* Discovering Doctrine *notebooks and their Book of Centuries entries.*

***Reminder:** Get* Men of Iron *for lesson 30 for grades 10–12.*

Book of Centuries Timeline

Lesson 21: Charlemagne

Materials Needed

- *A Castle with Many Rooms: The Story of the Middle Ages*
- A hammer or a picture of a hammer
- *The Story of King Arthur and His Knights* (grades 7–9)
- *The Lantern Bearers* (grades 10–12)

Family: Show students a hammer or a picture of a hammer and ask what they recall from last time's reading about Charles the Hammer and the Battle of Tours. Explain that today they will hear about Charles the Hammer's grandson, also named Charles. Write "Charles the Great" and "Charlemagne" on a small white board or sheet of paper for students to see. Read together *A Castle with Many Rooms: The Story of the Middle Ages,* chapter 9, "Charlemagne," and ask for an oral narration. Look together at the map on page 278 to see how Europe looked in 814, at the death of Charlemagne, or Charles the Great.

Charles the Great (Charlemagne), father of Europe (768–814)

Grades 7–9: Read together or assign as independent reading *The Story of King Arthur and His Knights,* "The Book of King Arthur," part III, chapter 3.

Grades 10–12: Assign as independent reading *The Lantern Bearers,* chapter 17, "Minnow, Dolphin's Son."

Lesson 22: Various History Readings

Materials Needed

- *Viking Adventure* (grades 1–3)
- *The Vikings* (grades 4–6)
- *The Story of King Arthur and His Knights* (grades 7–9)
- *Famous Men of the Middle Ages* (grades 10–12)
- *The Lantern Bearers* (grades 10–12)

Grades 1–3: Read together *Viking Adventure,* chapter 9, "The Stone."

Grades 4–6: Read together or assign as independent reading *The Vikings,*

Book of Centuries Timeline

Benedict the Monk (480–543)

Gregory the Monk and Gregorian chants (590–604)

the first half of chapter 5, "Leif's First Voyage."

Grades 7–9: Read together or assign as independent reading *The Story of King Arthur and His Knights,* "The Book of King Arthur," part III, chapter 4.

Grades 10–12: Read together or assign as independent reading *Famous Men of the Middle Ages,* chapter 9, "Benedict and Gregory," and ask for a written narration. Also assign as independent reading, *The Lantern Bearers,* chapter 18, "The Hostage."

Lesson 23: Visit 5 to Australia & James 5

Materials Needed

- *Visits to South & Central America and Australia*
- *Hungry Planet: What the World Eats*
- Bible
- James envelope and papers
- *Life in the Word* (grades 7–12)

Family Geography: Complete visit 5 in *Visits to South & Central America and Australia.*

Family Bible Study: Ask students what they recall about the epistle of James so far. Allow students to look at the James envelope and papers they have created to prompt review. Explain that today they will finish James' epistle with encouragement to keep the right perspective by looking at some examples of men from the Old Testament who endured trials.

Read together James 5, a paragraph at a time. Ask students to listen for the last of James' counsel about What To Do and What Not To Do in a trial. Pause after each paragraph and ask students to share what they discovered: verses 1–6, 7–11, 12–18, 19–20. Record students' suggestions on your ongoing papers.

Focus on James 5:10 and 11. What do you remember about Job's trials? (Review Job 1 as desired.) Discuss: How does it help to know that others have gone through hard times before us? Finish these sentences: The Lord is compassionate, which means that as I go through a hard time . . .; The Lord is merciful, which means that as I endure a trial . . . .

Grades 7–12: Help students to complete or assign as independent work *Life in the Word,* chapter 1, "Book Study of James," lesson 5.

Lesson 24: The Rushing North Wind

Materials Needed

- *A Castle with Many Rooms: The Story of the Middle Ages*
- *The Stuff They Left Behind: From the Days of the Middle Ages*

- *The Story of King Arthur and His Knights* (grades 7–9)
- *The Lantern Bearers* (grades 10–12)

Family: Display and discuss the picture of the Gokstad ship in *The Stuff They Left Behind: From the Days of the Middle Ages.* Help students locate "Northmen" on the map on page 278 of *A Castle with Many Rooms,* Europe at the Death of Charles the Great, and explain that this ship was discovered buried there. Read together *A Castle with Many Rooms: The Story of the Middle Ages,* chapter 10, "The Rushing North Wind," and ask for an oral narration.

Grades 7–9: Read together or assign as independent reading *The Story of King Arthur and His Knights,* "The Book of King Arthur," part III, chapter 5.

Grades 10–12: Assign as independent reading *The Lantern Bearers,* chapter 19, "Victory Like a Trumpet Blast."

Book of Centuries Timeline

Norsemen Vikings attack Lindisfarne (793)

Lesson 25: Various History Readings

Materials Needed

- *Viking Adventure* (grades 1–3)
- *The Vikings* (grades 4–6)
- *The Story of King Arthur and His Knights* (grades 7–9)
- *Famous Men of the Middle Ages* (grades 10–12)
- *The Lantern Bearers* (grades 10–12)

Grades 1–3: Read together *Viking Adventure,* chapter 10, "Aron."

Grades 4–6: Read together or assign as independent reading *The Vikings,* the last half of chapter 5, "Leif's First Voyage."

Grades 7–9: Read together or assign as independent reading *The Story of King Arthur and His Knights,* "The Book of King Arthur," part III, chapter 6.

Grades 10–12: Read together or assign as independent reading *Famous Men of the Middle Ages,* chapter 10, "Mohammed," and ask for a written narration. Also assign as independent reading, *The Lantern Bearers,* chapter 20, "The Dark Warrior."

***Tip:** Make sure older children are up to date with their* Discovering Doctrine *notebooks and their Book of Centuries entries.*

Lesson 26: The Meeting at Egbert's Stone

Materials Needed

- *A Castle with Many Rooms: The Story of the Middle Ages*

Book of Centuries Timeline

King Alfred defends Wessex from the Vikings (871–901)

- *The Story of King Arthur and His Knights,* if needed (grades 7–9)
- *The Lantern Bearers* (grades 10–12)

Family: Ask students what they recall from last time's reading about the Vikings. Read together *A Castle with Many Rooms: The Story of the Middle Ages,* chapter 11, "The Meeting at Egbert's Stone," referring to the maps of England on pages 276 and 277 as the story is read. Ask for an oral narration.

Grades 7–9: Use today to catch up and finish reading *The Story of King Arthur and His Knights,* "The Book of King Arthur," if needed.

Grades 10–12: Assign as independent reading *The Lantern Bearers,* chapter 21, "The Return of Odysseus."

Lesson 27: Various History Readings

Materials Needed
- *Viking Adventure* (grades 1–3)
- *The Vikings* (grades 4–6)
- *The Shining Company* (grades 7–9)
- *Famous Men of the Middle Ages* (grades 10–12)
- *The Lantern Bearers* (grades 10–12)

Grades 1–3: Read together *Viking Adventure,* chapter 11, "A Dream of Danger."

Grades 4–6: Read together or assign as independent reading *The Vikings,* the first half of chapter 6, "A Fight and a Stranger."

Grades 7–9: Read together or assign as independent reading *The Shining Company,* chapter 1, "The Brown Boy."

Grades 10–12: Read together or assign as independent reading *Famous Men of the Middle Ages,* chapter 11, "Charles Martel and Pepin," and ask for a written narration. Also assign as independent reading, *The Lantern Bearers,* chapter 22, "The Blossoming Tree."

Lesson 28: Visit 6 to Oceania & Galatians 1

Materials Needed
- *Visits to South & Central America and Australia*
- Bible
- Envelope with labeled paper inside
- Map of Paul's Journeys
- *Life in the Word* (grades 7–12)

Family Geography: Complete visit 6 in *Visits to South & Central America and Australia.*

Family Bible Study: Before the lesson begins, write the word *gospel* on a sheet of paper and put it inside an envelope. Ask students what they recall about the word *epistle* and how the epistles are named in the Bible. Explain that the next letter you will read is one that Paul wrote to several groups of believers in a large region called Galatia, so the epistle is called "To the Galatians," or just "Galatians." Display a map of "Paul's Journeys." (You should find one in a study Bible or in *Then and Now Bible Maps* if you have it from previous studies.) Help the students locate the region of Galatia. Compare it to a state or a province.

Help students address the envelope to reflect the epistle to the Galatians: put who it was from in the return address area and to whom it was written in the middle front. Have a student open the envelope and read the paper inside to find out what this letter is about.

Tip: *You may want to use different colored envelopes for the different epistles. Or you might allow the students to decorate the envelopes, if desired, or design a stamp to remind them of the theme of each epistle.*

Explain that Paul visited Galatia on his first missionary journey and many people in different towns of that region believed the gospel of Jesus Christ. (Those events are recorded in Acts 13 and 14.) Those believers included both Jews and Gentiles (non-Jewish people). Unfortunately, soon after Paul left to preach the gospel in other places, some men started telling those new believers that they must obey the Jewish religious laws or they weren't really right before God. When Paul heard about that false teaching, he wrote a letter to the Galatian believers to expose that error and teach them more about the freedom they had in Christ.

Explain that Paul talked a lot about "the gospel" in this epistle. *Gospel* means "good news"! Challenge students to listen carefully for what he said about the gospel as you read. He started off the letter exposing the false teaching the Galatian believers had recently been given and proving that he had been called by God to give them the true gospel. Read together Galatians 1 (or divide it into smaller portions over several days: verses 1–5, 6–10, 11–17, 18–24).

Focus on Galatians 1:10. Evidently, the false teachers had accused Paul of making up a message simply to please his hearers. Review what had actually happened when Paul was preaching the gospel in Galatia, in the town of Lystra, by reading Acts 14:19–23. How would you answer the questions Paul posed in Galatians 1:10? Why? We all want people to like us. What can we learn from Paul about that desire in this verse?

Ask students what they learned about the gospel in this chapter. Record their narrations on the sheet of paper and return it to the Galatians envelope for future lessons.

Grades 7–12: Help students to complete or assign as independent work *Life in the Word,* chapter 2, "Word Study on 'Faith,'" lesson 1.

Book of Centuries Timeline

Paul believes on Jesus (c. 33)

Paul's first missionary journey (46–47)

Paul writes his letter to the churches in Galatia (c. 48)

Book of Centuries Timeline

Lesson 29: Cornstalks and Quetzal Feathers

Materials Needed

- *A Castle with Many Rooms: The Story of the Middle Ages*
- *The Stuff They Left Behind: From the Days of the Middle Ages*
- *The Shining Company* (grades 7–9)
- *The Lantern Bearers*, if needed (grades 10–12)

Maya kingdoms disappear across Central America (900)

Family: Display and discuss the picture of El Castillo at Chichen Itza in *The Stuff They Left Behind: From the Days of the Middle Ages.* Help students locate Mexico on the world map (page 284 in *A Castle with Many Rooms*) and see where it is in relation to Europe. Write the word "Maya" on a small white board or sheet of paper so students can see it. Read together *A Castle with Many Rooms: The Story of the Middle Ages,* chapter 12, "Cornstalks and Quetzal Feathers." Display and discuss the picture of the Dresden Codex in *The Stuff They Left Behind: From the Days of the Middle Ages* as you read about it. Ask for an oral narration.

Grades 7–9: Read together or assign as independent reading *The Shining Company,* chapter 2, "The Archangel Dagger."

Grades 10–12: Use today to catch up and finish reading *The Lantern Bearers* if needed.

Lesson 30: Various History Readings

Materials Needed

- *Viking Adventure* (grades 1–3)
- *The Vikings* (grades 4–6)
- *The Shining Company* (grades 7–9)
- *Famous Men of the Middle Ages* (grades 10–12)
- *Men of Iron* (grades 10–12)

Grades 1–3: Read together *Viking Adventure,* chapter 12, "Fog and Storm."

Grades 4–6: Read together or assign as independent reading *The Vikings,* the last half of chapter 6, "A Fight and a Stranger."

Grades 7–9: Read together or assign as independent reading *The Shining Company,* chapter 3, "The White Hart."

Grades 10–12: Read together or assign as independent reading *Famous Men of the Middle Ages,* chapter 12, "Charlemagne," and ask for a written narration. Also assign as independent reading, *Men of Iron,* chapters 1 and 2.

***Tip:** Make sure older children are up to date with their* Discovering Doctrine *notebooks and their Book of Centuries entries.*

 Lesson 31: The Battle of Hastings

Materials Needed

- *A Castle with Many Rooms: The Story of the Middle Ages*
- *The Stuff They Left Behind: From the Days of the Middle Ages*
- *The Shining Company* (grades 7–9)
- *Men of Iron* (grades 10–12)

Family: Ask students what they recall from last time's reading about the Maya people in Mexico. Explain that today they will hear a story that happened about 100 years after the Maya people so mysteriously disappeared. This story takes place back across the sea near England. Read together *A Castle with Many Rooms: The Story of the Middle Ages,* chapter 13, "The Battle of Hastings," using the maps on pages 279 and 280 to help students follow the story. Ask for an oral narration. Display and discuss the picture of the Bayeux Tapestry in *The Stuff They Left Behind: From the Days of the Middle Ages.*

***Tip:** If desired, postpone the narration until after you have shown the picture of the tapestry. Omit the descriptions of the scenes in the discussion and, instead, challenge students to narrate the chapter by telling you about the scenes on that picture.*

Grades 7–9: Read together or assign as independent reading *The Shining Company,* chapter 4, "The Prince's Hunting."

Grades 10–12: Assign as independent reading *Men of Iron,* chapters 3 and 4.

 Lesson 32: Various History Readings

Materials Needed

- *Viking Adventure* (grades 1–3)
- *The Vikings* (grades 4–6)
- *The Shining Company* (grades 7–9)
- *Famous Men of the Middle Ages* (grades 10–12)
- *Men of Iron* (grades 10–12)

Grades 1–3: Read together *Viking Adventure,* chapter 13, "Remember This Day."

Grades 4–6: Read together or assign as independent reading *The Vikings,* the first half of chapter 7, "Leif the Lucky."

Grades 7–9: Read together or assign as independent reading *The Shining Company,* chapter 5, "The Summons."

Grades 10–12: Read together or assign as independent reading *Famous*

Book of Centuries Timeline

William, Duke of Normandy, defeats Harold Godwinson at the Battle of Hastings for the crown of England (1066)

Book of Centuries Timeline

Harun-al-Rashid, hero of the Arabian Nights stories (786–809)

Men of the Middle Ages, chapter 13, "Harun-al-Rashid," and ask for a written narration. Also assign as independent reading, *Men of Iron,* chapters 5 and 6.

Lesson 33: Visit 7 to Oceania & Galatians 2

Materials Needed

- *Visits to South & Central America and Australia*
- Bible
- Galatians envelope and paper
- *Life in the Word* (grades 7–12)

Family Geography: Complete visit 7 in *Visits to South & Central America and Australia.*

Family Bible Study: Display the Galatians envelope from last time's Family Bible Study. Ask students what they recall about Paul's letter to the Galatians and the circumstances that prompted it. Remind students that Paul was telling the story of how he became an apostle of Jesus Christ and took the good news ("gospel") to the Gentiles (non-Jewish people).

Tell students to listen carefully for what he said about the gospel message as you read. Read together Galatians 2 (or divide it into smaller portions over several days: verses 1–10, 11–14, 15–21).

Tip: *The Jewish law commanded that all Jewish boys should be circumcised—a physical mark that symbolized their position as God's chosen people. Yet a person could have that physical mark and still turn away from God in his heart. The physical action of receiving that mark did not make his heart right.*

Focus on Galatians 2:15 and 16. Write the word "justified" on a small white board or sheet of paper; explain that it means "declared right before God." Discuss: According to these verses, how is a person justified? How is a person not justified? What kinds of physical works do people today do to try to achieve a right standing before God? Can those actions guarantee that their hearts are right? Why? What is the gospel message of these verses?

Ask students what good news they learned in this chapter. Record their narrations on the sheet of paper and return it to the Galatians envelope for future lessons.

Grades 7–12: Help students to complete or assign as independent work *Life in the Word,* chapter 2, "Word Study on 'Faith,'" lesson 2.

Lesson 34: Feudalism

Materials Needed

- *A Castle with Many Rooms: The Story of the Middle Ages*

Book of Centuries Timeline

- *The Shining Company* (grades 7–9)
- *Men of Iron* (grades 10–12)

Family: Ask students what they recall from last time's reading about the Battle of Hastings and how William the Conqueror changed England. Explain that today they will hear about one of the biggest changes William brought to England: feudalism. Write "feudalism" on a small white board or sheet of paper for students to see. Read together *A Castle with Many Rooms: The Story of the Middle Ages,* chapter 14, "Feudalism," and ask for an oral narration.

Grades 7–9: Read together or assign as independent reading *The Shining Company,* chapter 6, "The Golden King and the Three Hundred."

Grades 10–12: Assign as independent reading *Men of Iron,* chapters 7 and 8.

Lesson 35: Various History Readings

Materials Needed

- *Viking Adventure* (grades 1–3)
- *The Vikings* (grades 4–6)
- *The Shining Company* (grades 7–9)
- *Famous Men of the Middle Ages* (grades 10–12)
- *Men of Iron* (grades 10–12)

Grades 1–3: Read together *Viking Adventure,* chapter 14, "A String of Shells."

Grades 4–6: Read together or assign as independent reading *The Vikings,* the last half of chapter 7, "Leif the Lucky."

Grades 7–9: Read together or assign as independent reading *The Shining Company,* chapter 7, "The Gathering Feast."

Grades 10–12: Read together or assign as independent reading *Famous Men of the Middle Ages,* chapter 14, "Egbert the Saxon," and ask for a written narration. Also assign as independent reading, *Men of Iron,* chapters 9 and 10.

Tip: *Make sure older children are up to date with their* Discovering Doctrine *notebooks and their Book of Centuries entries.*

Lesson 36: The Way of the Warrior

Materials Needed

- *A Castle with Many Rooms: The Story of the Middle Ages*
- *The Stuff They Left Behind: From the Days of the Middle Ages*
- *The Shining Company* (grades 7–9)
- *Men of Iron* (grades 10–12)

Book of Centuries Timeline

Shoguns (military leaders) dominate Japan (1170–1868)

Family: Ask students what they recall from last time's reading about feudalism. Explain that Europe was not the only place with kings and nobles, knights and warriors. Help students locate Japan on the world map (page 284 in *A Castle with Many Rooms*). Explain that Japan had many of the same positions of people; they just had different names. Read together *A Castle with Many Rooms: The Story of the Middle Ages,* chapter 15, "The Way of the Warrior." Display and discuss the picture of Armor in *The Stuff They Left Behind: From the Days of the Middle Ages* as you read about the Japanese samurai and the European knights. Ask for an oral narration of similarities and differences.

Grades 7–9: Read together or assign as independent reading *The Shining Company,* chapter 8, "The Swordsmith."

Grades 10–12: Assign as independent reading *Men of Iron,* chapter 11.

Reminder: *Get* Castle *for lesson 46.*

Lesson 37: Various History Readings

Materials Needed

- *Viking Adventure* (grades 1–3)
- *The Vikings* (grades 4–6)
- *The Shining Company* (grades 7–9)
- *Famous Men of the Middle Ages* (grades 10–12)
- *Men of Iron* (grades 10–12)

Grades 1–3: Read together *Viking Adventure,* chapter 15, "The Cliff."

Grades 4–6: Read together or assign as independent reading *The Vikings,* the first half of chapter 8, "To the West!"

Grades 7–9: Read together or assign as independent reading *The Shining Company,* chapter 9, "Ordeal by Wakefulness."

Rollo the Viking acquires Normandy in France (c. 860–932)

Grades 10–12: Read together or assign as independent reading *Famous Men of the Middle Ages,* chapter 15, "Rollo the Viking," and ask for a written narration. Also assign as independent reading, *Men of Iron,* chapters 12 and 13.

Lesson 38: Visit 8 to Oceania & Galatians 3

Materials Needed

- *Visits to South & Central America and Australia*

- Bible
- Galatians envelope and paper
- *Life in the Word* (grades 7–12)

Family Geography: Complete visit 8 in *Visits to South & Central America and Australia.*

Family Bible Study: Display the Galatians envelope and paper. Ask students what they recall about the good news that Paul preached to the Gentiles. Read Galatians 2:15 and 16 to prompt the review as needed. Explain that the next part of Paul's letter would explain *why* keeping the law was not the way to become right before God (to be justified).

Read together Galatians 3 (or divide it into smaller portions over several days: verses 1–9, 10–14, 15–18, 19–29).

Tip: *Abraham was considered the father of the Jews; God selected Abraham when he was 75 years old and promised that his descendants would become God's chosen people (in Genesis 12 and 15). That acceptance from God was not based on Abraham's being circumcised, however, for God did not tell him to do that until 24 years later, when Abraham was 99 years old (in Genesis 17).*

Explain that just as a schoolmaster/teacher helps us discover what we don't know (how ignorant we are), so the law helped people discover how sinful they were. It showed people their need of Jesus Christ to save them from their sins.

Focus on Galatians 3:28. Discuss: In what ways can jobs and gender and ethnicity cause divisions among people? Why do those things not matter to the gospel message? We may have different roles and responsibilities in life, but how are believers "all one in Christ Jesus"?

Ask students what they learned about the gospel in this chapter. Record their narrations on the sheet of paper and return it to the Galatians envelope for future lessons.

Grades 7–12: Help students to complete or assign as independent work *Life in the Word,* chapter 3, "Topical Study on Freedom," lesson 1.

Book of Centuries Timeline

 Lesson 39: The Cross upon the Shield

Materials Needed

- *A Castle with Many Rooms: The Story of the Middle Ages*
- *The Shining Company* (grades 7–9)
- *Men of Iron* (grades 10–12)

Family: Ask students what they recall from last time's reading about warriors in the Middle Ages. Explain that in today's reading they will learn about a challenge that many European knights accepted and fought for. Read together *A Castle with Many Rooms: The Story of the Middle Ages,*

Christians fight Muslims for Jerusalem in First Crusade (1096–1099)

Book of Centuries Timeline

chapter 16, "The Cross Upon the Shield." Use the map on page 281, Era of the Crusades, to help students follow the story. Ask for an oral narration.

Grades 7–9: Read together or assign as independent reading *The Shining Company,* chapter 10, "The Night of the Running Wolves."

Grades 10–12: Assign as independent reading *Men of Iron,* chapters 14 and 15.

 Lesson 40: Various History Readings

Materials Needed

- *Viking Adventure* (grades 1–3)
- *The Vikings* (grades 4–6)
- *The Shining Company*, if needed (grades 7–9)
- *Famous Men of the Middle Ages* (grades 10–12)
- *Men of Iron* (grades 10–12)

Grades 1–3: Read together *Viking Adventure,* chapter 16, "The Knife."

Grades 4–6: Read together or assign as independent reading *The Vikings,* the last half of chapter 8, "To the West!"

Grades 7–9: Use today to catch up on any assigned reading so far in *The Shining Company* if needed.

Henry the Fowler defends Germany from the Magyars (919–936)

Grades 10–12: Read together or assign as independent reading *Famous Men of the Middle Ages,* chapter 16, "Henry the Fowler," and ask for a written narration. Also assign as independent reading, *Men of Iron,* chapters 16 and 17.

***Tip:** Make sure older children are up to date with their* Discovering Doctrine *notebooks and their Book of Centuries entries.*

 Lesson 41: Lionheart and Robin Hood

Materials Needed

- *A Castle with Many Rooms: The Story of the Middle Ages*
- *The Shining Company* (grades 7–9)
- *Men of Iron* (grades 10–12)

Richard the Lionheart makes peace treaty with Saladin at Third Crusade (1192)

Robin Hood fights the injustice of Prince John (1192–1194)

Family: Ask students what they recall from last time's reading about the first crusade. Read together *A Castle with Many Rooms: The Story of the Middle Ages,* chapter 17, "Lionheart and Robin Hood." Use the map on page 281, Era of the Crusades, to help students follow the story. Ask for an oral narration.

Grades 7–9: Read together or assign as independent reading *The Shining Company,* chapter 11, "The Champion's Portion."

Grades 10–12: Assign as independent reading *Men of Iron,* chapter 18.

Book of Centuries Timeline

Lesson 42: Various History Readings

Materials Needed

- *Viking Adventure* (grades 1–3)
- *The Vikings* (grades 4–6)
- *The Shining Company* (grades 7–9)
- *Famous Men of the Middle Ages* (grades 10–12)
- *Men of Iron* (grades 10–12)

Grades 1–3: Read together *Viking Adventure,* chapter 17, "On the Steering Deck."

Grades 4–6: Read together or assign as independent reading *The Vikings,* the first half of chapter 9, "Vineland the Good."

Grades 7–9: Read together or assign as independent reading *The Shining Company,* chapter 12, "Epona's Leap."

Grades 10–12: Read together or assign as independent reading *Famous Men of the Middle Ages,* chapter 17, "Alfred the Great," and ask for a written narration. Also assign as independent reading, *Men of Iron,* chapter 19.

Lesson 43: Visit 9 to Oceania & Galatians 4

Materials Needed

- *Visits to South & Central America and Australia*
- *Material World*
- Bible
- Galatians envelope and paper
- *Life in the Word* (grades 7–12)

Family Geography: Complete visit 9 in *Visits to South & Central America and Australia.*

Family Bible Study: Display the Galatians envelope and paper. Ask students what they recall from Galatians about the gospel message and how a person is accepted by God. Explain that Paul was about to give a beautiful picture of what happens when a person believes the gospel: he is adopted into God's family. He is no longer a slave to the law but has become a child of God and a rightful heir.

Read together Galatians 4 (or divide it into smaller portions over several

Book of Centuries Timeline

days: verses 1–7, 8–11, 12–20, 21–31).

Tip: Paul used an allegory taken from the event recorded in Genesis 16. God promised Abraham that his descendants would come through a son. Abraham faltered in his faith and had a son with Hagar, a slave, but that was not God's way. The son that Abraham had with his wife, Sarah, was the son whose descendants would become God's chosen people. Paul then compared Hagar and her child to those born as slaves to the law, but Sarah and her child represent those born as true sons and heirs.

Focus on Galatians 4:4–7. Discuss: The law revealed our sin and there was nothing we could do to pay for that sin. But what did God do for us? What is the difference between a slave and a son? What is the difference between viewing God as your slavedriver and viewing Him as your Father? That's the good news of the gospel!

Ask students what they learned about the gospel in this chapter. Record their narrations on the sheet of paper and return it to the Galatians envelope for future lessons.

Grades 7–12: Help students to complete or assign as independent work *Life in the Word,* chapter 3, "Topical Study on Freedom," lesson 2.

Lesson 44: Castles

Materials Needed

- *A Castle with Many Rooms: The Story of the Middle Ages*
- *The Stuff They Left Behind: From the Days of the Middle Ages*
- *The Shining Company* (grades 7–9)
- *Men of Iron* (grades 10–12)

Family: Ask students what they recall from last time's reading about the crusades and King Richard the Lionheart. Display and discuss the picture of the Krak de Chaveliers in *The Stuff They Left Behind: From the Days of the Middle Ages.* Read together *A Castle with Many Rooms: The Story of the Middle Ages,* chapter 18, "Castles," and ask for an oral narration.

Grades 7–9: Read together or assign as independent reading *The Shining Company,* chapter 13, "The Rider from the South."

Grades 10–12: Assign as independent reading *Men of Iron,* chapters 20 and 21.

Lesson 45: Various History Readings

Materials Needed

- *Viking Adventure* (grades 1–3)

- *The Vikings* (grades 4–6)
- *The Shining Company* (grades 7–9)
- *Famous Men of the Middle Ages* (grades 10–12)
- *Men of Iron* (grades 10–12)

Grades 1–3: Read together *Viking Adventure,* chapter 18, "Sigurd and Aron."

Grades 4–6: Read together or assign as independent reading *The Vikings,* the last half of chapter 9, "Vineland the Good."

Grades 7–9: Read together or assign as independent reading *The Shining Company,* chapter 14, "The Road to Catraeth."

Grades 10–12: Read together or assign as independent reading *Famous Men of the Middle Ages,* chapter 18, "Canute the Great," and ask for a written narration. Also assign as independent reading, *Men of Iron,* chapter 22.

Tip: Make sure older children are up to date with their Discovering Doctrine *notebooks and their Book of Centuries entries.*

Book of Centuries Timeline

Canute the Great, Danish king of England (1016–1035)

 Lesson 46: More About Castles, part 1

Materials Needed
- *Castle*
- *The Shining Company* (grades 7–9)
- *Men of Iron* (grades 10–12)

Family: Ask students what they recall from last time's reading about castles. Explain that over the next few readings they will get to watch as a castle is built and see all that goes into its construction. Read together *Castle,* pages 6–15.

Tip: As an alternate to an oral narration, you might allow the children to build a model castle, draw a plan for a castle, or build a castle out of blocks, based on what they learn from the book.

Grades 7–9: Read together or assign as independent reading *The Shining Company,* chapter 15, "Night Attack."

Grades 10–12: Assign as independent reading *Men of Iron,* chapter 23.

 Lesson 47: Various History Readings

Materials Needed
- *Viking Adventure* (grades 1–3)

Book of Centuries Timeline

- *The Vikings* (grades 4–6)
- *The Shining Company* (grades 7–9)
- *Famous Men of the Middle Ages* (grades 10–12)
- *Men of Iron* (grades 10–12)

Grades 1–3: Read together *Viking Adventure,* chapter 19, "A Light on the Island."

Grades 4–6: Read together or assign as independent reading *The Vikings,* the first half of chapter 10, "Greenland Is My Home."

Grades 7–9: Read together or assign as independent reading *The Shining Company,* chapter 16, "Waiting for Elmet."

Edward the Confessor drives Macbeth out of Scotland; builds Westminster Abbey (1042–1066)

Grades 10–12: Read together or assign as independent reading *Famous Men of the Middle Ages,* chapter 19, "Edward the Confessor," and ask for a written narration. Also assign as independent reading, *Men of Iron,* chapter 24.

Lesson 48: Visit 10 to Oceania & Galatians 5

Materials Needed

- *Visits to South & Central America and Australia*
- Bible
- Galatians envelope and paper
- *Life in the Word* (grades 7–12)

Family Geography: Complete visit 10 in *Visits to South & Central America and Australia.*

Family Bible Study: Display the Galatians envelope and paper. Ask students what they recall from Galatians about the gospel message and how it changes us from being a slave to being a child in God's family. Explain that God has sent His Spirit into our hearts to help us live like a member of His family, like a child of God.

Read together Galatians 5 (or divide it into smaller portions over several days: verses 1–6, 7–12, 13–15, 16–26).

Focus on Galatians 5:13–15. Discuss: Now that we are no longer slaves, how should we use our new freedom? How should we not use it? Do you recall anyone else in the Bible saying that "love your neighbor as yourself" sums up the law? (See Matthew 22:36–40 and Mark 12:30 and 31.) How does that one guideline sum up all the laws for God's family?

Ask students what good news they learned in this chapter. Record their narrations on the sheet of paper and return it to the envelope for future lessons.

Grades 7–12: Help students to complete or assign as independent work *Life* *in the Word,* chapter 3, "Topical Study on Freedom," lesson 3.

Book of Centuries Timeline

 Lesson 49: More About Castles, part 2

Materials Needed

- *Castle*
- *The Shining Company* (grades 7–9)
- *Men of Iron* (grades 10–12)

Family: Use the illustrations on pages 6–15 of *Castle* to briefly review how far the castle was constructed last time, then read together pages 16–27.

Grades 7–9: Read together or assign as independent reading *The Shining Company,* chapter 17, "The Last Day."

Grades 10–12: Assign as independent reading *Men of Iron,* chapters 25 and 26.

***Reminder:** If you want to do an optional hands-on project for lessons 56–60, start collecting the materials you will need.*

 Lesson 50: Various History Readings

Materials Needed

- *Viking Adventure* (grades 1–3)
- *The Vikings* (grades 4–6)
- *The Shining Company* (grades 7–9)
- *Famous Men of the Middle Ages* (grades 10–12)
- *Men of Iron* (grades 10–12)

Grades 1–3: Read together *Viking Adventure,* chapter 20, "The Hut."

Grades 4–6: Read together or assign as independent reading *The Vikings,* the last half of chapter 10, "Greenland Is My Home."

Grades 7–9: Read together or assign as independent reading *The Shining Company,* chapter 18, "The Shining Company."

Grades 10–12: Read together or assign as independent reading *Famous Men of the Middle Ages,* chapter 20, "William the Conqueror," and ask for a written narration. Also assign as independent reading, *Men of Iron,* chapters 27 and 28.

***Tip:** Make sure older children are up to date with their* Discovering Doctrine *notebooks and their Book of Centuries entries.*

Book of Centuries Timeline

Reminder: *Start gathering the resources you will need for Term 2. See page 53.*

 Lesson 51: More About Castles, part 3

Materials Needed

- *Castle*
- *The Shining Company* (grades 7–9)
- *Men of Iron* (grades 10–12)

Family: Use the illustrations on pages 16–27 of *Castle* to briefly review how far the castle was constructed last time, then read together pages 28–43.

Grades 7–9: Read together or assign as independent reading *The Shining Company,* chapter 19, "The Road Back."

Grades 10–12: Assign as independent reading *Men of Iron,* chapters 29 and 30.

 Lesson 52: Various History Readings

Materials Needed

- *Viking Adventure* (grades 1–3)
- *The Vikings* (grades 4–6)
- *The Shining Company* (grades 7–9)
- *Famous Men of the Middle Ages* (grades 10–12)
- *Men of Iron* (grades 10–12)

Grades 1–3: Read together *Viking Adventure,* chapter 21, "Sigurd's Story."

Grades 4–6: Read together or assign as independent reading *The Vikings,* the first half of chapter 11, "Karlsefni's Voyage."

Grades 7–9: Read together or assign as independent reading *The Shining Company,* chapter 20, "Ghosts."

El Cid (Rodrigo Diaz de Bivar), knight of Christian Spain, performs many exploits against the Spanish Moors (1044–1099)

Grades 10–12: Read together or assign as independent reading *Famous Men of the Middle Ages,* chapter 21, "El Cid," and ask for a written narration. Also assign as independent reading, *Men of Iron,* chapters 31 and 32.

 Lesson 53: Visit 11 to Oceania & Galatians 6

Materials Needed

- *Visits to South & Central America and Australia*
- Bible

- Galatians envelope and paper
- *Life in the Word* (grades 7–12)

Family Geography: Complete visit 11 in *Visits to South & Central America and Australia.*

Family Bible Study: Display the Galatians envelope and paper. Ask students what they recall from Galatians about living like a child of God. See if they remember the guideline that sums up the whole law. (Love your neighbor as yourself.) Explain that Paul finished this epistle by encouraging the Galatians to take care of each other and emphasizing again that keeping the law and getting the physical mark of circumcision is not the good news of the gospel.

Read together Galatians 6 (or divide it into smaller portions over several days: verses 1–5, 6–10, 11–18).

Focus on Galatians 6:9 and 10. Discuss: What might cause us to grow weary in doing good? Who is the "household of faith"? How does verse 10 reflect the one guideline that sums up the whole law?

Ask students what they learned in this chapter. Record their narrations on the sheet of paper and return it to the Galatians envelope.

Grades 7–12: Help students to complete or assign as independent work *Life in the Word,* chapter 4, "Doctrine Study."

Book of Centuries Timeline

 Lesson 54: More About Castles, part 4

Materials Needed

- *Castle*
- *The Shining Company* (grades 7–9)
- *Men of Iron* (grades 10–12)

Family: Use the illustrations on pages 28–43 of *Castle* to briefly review how far the castle was constructed last time, then read together pages 44–55.

Tip: *You will finish reading* Castle *after exam week.*

Grades 7–9: Read together or assign as independent reading *The Shining Company,* chapter 21, "The Flower of an Emperor's Bodyguard."

Grades 10–12: Assign as independent reading *Men of Iron,* chapter 33 and the Conclusion.

 Lesson 55: Various History Readings

Materials Needed

- *Viking Adventure,* if needed (grades 1–3)

Book of Centuries Timeline

- *The Vikings* (grades 4–6)
- *The Shining Company*, if needed (grades 7–9)
- *Famous Men of the Middle Ages* (grades 10–12)
- *Men of Iron*, if needed (grades 10–12)

Grades 1–3: Use today to catch up and finish any reading in *Viking Adventure* as needed.

Grades 4–6: Read together or assign as independent reading *The Vikings,* the last half of chapter 11, "Karlsefni's Voyage."

Grades 7–9: Use today to catch up and finish reading *The Shining Company* if needed.

Pope Gregory VII and Emperor Henry IV battle for power (1073–1105)

Grades 10–12: Read together or assign as independent reading *Famous Men of the Middle Ages,* chapter 22, "Pope Gregory VII and Emperor Henry IV," and ask for a written narration. Also use today to catch up and finish reading *Men of Iron* if needed.

***Tip:** Make sure older children are up to date with their* Discovering Doctrine *notebooks and their Book of Centuries entries.*

Lesson 56: History Catch Up, Exam, or Project

Materials Needed

- *The Stuff They Left Behind: From the Days of the Middle Ages*
- (optional) Materials for hands-on project

Family: Use today to catch up on any history reading you need to finish, or use the questions below for the students' exam on Middle Ages history studied so far. You may also use the history lessons this week to do an optional hands-on project if you would prefer.

***Tip:** Exams in a Charlotte Mason school require no "cramming" or preparation. You may be pleasantly surprised at what your students remember with no prompting.*

Grades 1–3: Display these four pictures from *The Stuff They Left Behind: From the Days of the Middle Ages* portfolio: the Gokstad Viking ship, El Castillo, Bayeux Tapestry, Crusader castle. Invite your student to select one of the pictures and tell the story about it. (For example, he could tell about Vikings, about the Maya, about the Battle of Hastings, or about castles or the crusades.)
Grades 4–6: Select two names from the list of men with nicknames, on page 52 of this book, and tell the story of each.

Grades 7–9: Tell about a Middle Ages event you have read about that occurred (a) west of England and (b) in England.
Grades 10–12: Tell all you know about feudalism: how it came into being, how it worked, its advantages and disadvantages, and the role it played during the Middle Ages.

Tip: You may want to assign the older students to write their exam answers. Younger students may do oral exams; you might want to write or type their answers as they tell what they know. Or, if you have students in more than one grade level, you might allow them to do their exams orally in a group. That way the older can hear the younger, and the younger can hear the older.

Optional Hands-On Project: Select a hands-on project from the Links and Tips page at http://simplycm.com/middle-ages-links.

Lesson 57: History Catch Up, Exam, or Project

Materials Needed

- (optional) Materials for hands-on project

Family: Use today to catch up on any history reading you need to finish, or use the questions below for the students' exam on Middle Ages history studied so far. You may also do an optional hands-on project.
Grades 1–3: Tell the story of an explorer you read about this term.
Grades 4–6: Select two more names from the list of men with nicknames, on page 52 of this book, and tell the story of each.
Grades 7–9: Tell about a Middle Ages event you have read about that occurred (a) east of England and west of Italy and (b) east of Italy.
Grades 10–12: The author of *A Castle with Many Rooms* described the Battle of Tours as "one of history's great hinges." Explain what that term means, what the Battle of Tours was, and why it could be characterized that way.

Optional Hands-On Project: Continue your selected hands-on project or start a new one if desired.

Lesson 58: Visit 12 to Oceania & Bible Exam

Materials Needed

- *Visits to South & Central America and Australia*

Family Geography: Complete visit 12 in *Visits to South & Central America and Australia.*

Book of Centuries Timeline

Book of Centuries Timeline

Family Bible Exam: Use today to catch up on any Bible reading you need to finish, or use the questions below for the students' exam on the epistles studied so far.
Family: Tell what you know about the epistle of James and its emphasis on enduring trials. And/or tell what you know about the epistle to the Galatians and its emphasis on the gospel.

Tip: *It is up to you whether to ask your students to summarize one or both epistles that were studied.*

Grades 7–12: Write (a) a summary of the book of James, chapter by chapter; (b) a description of your findings for the word study on "faith" in Galatians; (c) a description of your findings for the topical study on freedom in Galatians. What did you study and what did you learn?

Lesson 59: History Catch Up, Exam, or Project

Materials Needed

- (optional) Materials for hands-on project

Family: Use today to catch up on any history reading you need to finish, or use the questions below for the students' exam on Middle Ages history studied so far.
Grades 1–3: Tell your favorite story about the Middle Ages so far.
Grades 4–6: Select two more names from the list of men with nicknames, on page 52 of this book, and tell the story of each.
Grades 7–9: Select two of the following quotes; for each of them tell who said it and the events surrounding it: (a) "Vestrum est, Britanni, vos ipsos defendere." ("It is your own task, Britons, to defend yourselves."); (b) "We go to England."; (c) "Deus vult!" (God wills it!)
Grades 10–12: Several men who lived in Medieval times earned the nickname "the Great": (a) Justinian, (b) Charlemagne, (c) King Alfred, (d) Canute, (e) Roderick (El Cid). Select three and tell what you know about each, describing what made people consider him great, how you would define greatness, and whether you think he deserved that title. Support your opinion with examples from the history you read.

Optional Hands-On Project: Continue your selected hands-on project or start a new one if desired.

Lesson 60: History Catch Up, Exam, or Project

Materials Needed

- *The Stuff They Left Behind: From the Days of the Middle Ages*

- (optional) Materials for hands-on project

Family: Use today to catch up on any history reading you need to finish, or use the questions below for the students' exam on Middle Ages history studied so far.
Grades 1–3: Display these four pictures from *The Stuff They Left Behind: From the Days of the Middle Ages* portfolio: the Gokstad Viking ship, El Castillo, Bayeux Tapestry, Crusader castle. Invite your student to select a picture he has not yet told about and tell the story about it. (He could tell about Vikings, about the Maya, about the Battle of Hastings, or about castles or the crusades.)
Grades 4–6: Describe how a castle was designed and why.
Grades 7–9: Explain two of these institutions and describe their place in the Medieval world: (a) feudalism, (b) castles, (c) monasteries.
Grades 10–12: Draw a detailed sketch or write an essay that surveys the world during the Middle Ages. Include the key people and events that happened in the following regions: (a) Asia, (b) Africa, (c) the Middle East, (d) southern Europe, (e) northern Europe, (f) Britain, (g) South and Central America, (h) North America.

Optional Hands-On Project: Finish your selected hands-on project.

Book of Centuries Timeline

Middle Ages Men with Nicknames

- Justinian the Great
- Brendan the Navigator
- Erik the Red
- Charles the Hammer
- Charles the Great (Charlemagne)
- Alfred the Great
- William the Conqueror
- Richard the Lionheart

Term 2

(12 weeks; 5 lessons/week)

Term 2 Book List

Family

- *Around the World in a Hundred Years* by Jean Fritz
- Bible
- *Castle* by David Macaulay
- *A Castle with Many Rooms: The Story of the Middle Ages* by Lorene Lambert
- *Cathedral* by David Macaulay
- *Material World* **and** *Hungry Planet: What the World Eats* by Peter Menzel
- *The Stuff They Left Behind: From the Days of the Middle Ages* portfolio
- *Visits to South & Central America and Australia* notebook by Sonya Shafer (one for each student)

Plus . . .

Grades 1–3

- *Brother Francis and the Friendly Beasts* by Margaret Hodges
- *Medieval Feast* by Aliki
- *The Sword in the Tree* by Clyde Robert Bulla

Grades 4–6

- *Adam of the Road* by Elizabeth Janet Gray
- *King Arthur and His Knights* audio recording by Jim Weiss
- "The Pied Piper of Hamelin" poem by Robert Browning

Grades 7–9

- Book of Centuries (one for each student)
- *Discovering Doctrine* by Sonya Shafer (one for each student)
- *In Freedom's Cause* by G. A. Henty
- *Life in the Word* by Sonya Shafer (one for each student)
- *The Magna Charta* by James Daugherty

Grades 10–12

- *The Black Arrow* by Robert Louis Stevenson
- Book of Centuries (one for each student)
- *Discovering Doctrine* by Sonya Shafer (one for each student)
- *Famous Men of the Middle Ages,* with extra chapters by Rob Shearer (2008 edition, published by Greenleaf Press)
- *Famous Men of the Renaissance and Reformation* by Rob Shearer
- *Life in the Word* by Sonya Shafer (one for each student)
- *Voices of the Renaissance and Reformation* by Rob Shearer

What You Will Cover As a Family

History: *From the Magna Carta through the beginning of the Renaissance (1200–1469)*

Geography: *Medieval Europe; South America*

Bible: *1 and 2 Thessalonians and part of 1 Corinthians*

Term 2 At a Glance

	Family	Grades 1-3	Grades 4-6	Grades 7-9	Grades 10-12
			Week 1, Lessons 61-65		
History	Castle, parts 5, 6	The Sword in the Tree, ch. 1, 2	King Arthur and His Knights audio	The Magna Charta, parts 1-6	Famous Men of the Middle Ages, ch. 23, 24; The Black Arrow, Prologue, Book I, ch. 1-3
Geography	Visits to South and Central America, Australia, Visit 13				
Bible	1 Thessalonians 1, 2			Life in the Word, ch. 5, lesson 1	Life in the Word, ch. 5, lesson 1
			Week 2, Lessons 66-70		
History	A Castle with Many Rooms, ch. 19, 20	The Sword in the Tree, ch. 3, 4	The Pied Piper; Adam of the Road, ch. 1	The Magna Charta, parts 7-14	Famous Men of the Middle Ages, ch. 25, 26; The Black Arrow, Book I, ch. 4-7
Geography	Visits to South and Central America, Australia, Visit 14				
Bible	1 Thessalonians 3, 4			Life in the Word, ch. 5, lesson 2	Life in the Word, ch. 5, lesson 2
			Week 3, Lessons 71-75		
History	A Castle with Many Rooms, ch. 21, 22	The Sword in the Tree, ch. 5, 6	Adam of the Road, ch. 2	The Magna Charta, parts 15-22	Famous Men of the Middle Ages, ch. 27, 28; The Black Arrow, Book II, ch. 1-3
Geography	Visits to South and Central America, Australia, Visit 15				
Bible	1 Thessalonians 5			Life in the Word, ch. 6, lesson 1	Life in the Word, ch. 6, lesson 1
			Week 4, Lessons 76-80		
History	Cathedral, parts 1, 2	The Sword in the Tree, ch. 7, 8	Adam of the Road, ch. 3, 4A	The Magna Charta, parts 23-32	Famous Men of the Middle Ages, ch. 29, 30; The Black Arrow, Book II, ch. 4-5, Book III, ch. 1
Geography	Visits to South and Central America, Australia, Visit 16				
Bible	2 Thessalonians 1, 2			Life in the Word, ch. 6, lesson 2	Life in the Word, ch. 6, lesson 2
			Week 5, Lessons 81-85		
History	Cathedral, parts 3, 4	The Sword in the Tree, ch. 9, 10	Adam of the Road, ch. 4B, 5A	In Freedom's Cause, ch. 1-4	Famous Men of the Middle Ages, ch. 31, 32; The Black Arrow, Book III, ch. 2-5
Geography	Visits to South and Central America, Australia, Visit 17				
Bible	2 Thessalonians 3			Life in the Word, ch. 6, lesson 3	Life in the Word, ch. 6, lesson 3
			Week 6, Lessons 86-90		
History	Cathedral, part 5; A Castle with Many Rooms, ch. 23	The Sword in the Tree, ch. 11, 12	Adam of the Road, ch. 5B, 6A	In Freedom's Cause, ch. 5-8	Famous Men of the Middle Ages, ch. 33, 34; The Black Arrow, Book III, ch. 6, Book IV, ch. 1, 2
Geography	Visits to South and Central America, Australia, Visit 18				
Bible	1 Corinthians 1			Life in the Word, ch. 6, lesson 4	Life in the Word, ch. 6, lesson 4

Use this chart to see what your family and each of your students will be studying week by week during this term. You will also be able to see when each book is scheduled to be used.

	Family	Grades 1-3	Grades 4-6	Grades 7-9	Grades 10-12
Week 7, Lessons 91–95					
History	A Castle with Many Rooms, ch. 24, 25	The Sword in the Tree, ch. 13, 14	Adam of the Road, ch. 6B, 7A	In Freedom's Cause, ch. 9–12	Famous Men of the Middle Ages, ch. 35, 36; The Black Arrow, Book IV, ch. 3–6
Geography	Visits to South and Central America, Australia, Visit 19				
Bible	1 Corinthians 2, 3			Life in the Word, ch. 7, lesson 1	Life in the Word, ch. 7, lesson 1
Week 8, Lessons 96–100					
History	A Castle with Many Rooms, ch. 26; Around the World in 100 Years, ch. 3	Brother Francis and the Friendly Beasts, part 1	Adam of the Road, ch. 7B, 8A	In Freedom's Cause, ch. 13–16	Famous Men of the Ren and Ref, ch. 1; Voices; The Black Arrow, Book V, ch. 1–3
Geography	Visits to South and Central America, Australia, Visit 20				
Bible	1 Corinthians 4, 5			Life in the Word, ch. 7, lesson 2	Life in the Word, ch. 7, lesson 2
Week 9, Lessons 101–105					
History	Around the World in 100 Years, ch. 4, 5	Brother Francis and the Friendly Beasts, parts 2, 3	Adam of the Road, ch. 8B, 9A	In Freedom's Cause, ch. 17–20	Famous Men of the Ren and Ref, ch. 2, 3; The Black Arrow, Book V, ch. 4–7
Geography	Visits to South and Central America, Australia, Visit 21				
Bible	1 Corinthians 6, 7			Life in the Word, ch. 7, lesson 3	Life in the Word, ch. 7, lesson 3
Week 10, Lessons 106–110					
History	Around the World in 100 Years, ch. 6, 7	Brother Francis and the Friendly Beasts, part 4	Adam of the Road, ch. 9B, 10A	In Freedom's Cause, ch. 21–24	Famous Men of the Ren and Ref, ch. 4, 5; Voices; The Black Arrow, Book V, ch. 8
Geography	Visits to South and Central America, Australia, Visit 22				
Bible	1 Corinthians 8, 9			Life in the Word, ch. 7, lesson 4	Life in the Word, ch. 7, lesson 4
Week 11, Lessons 111–115					
History	Around the World in 100 Years, ch. 8, 9	A Medieval Feast	Adam of the Road, ch. 10B, 11	In Freedom's Cause, ch. 25–27	Famous Men of the Ren and Ref, ch. 6, 7; Voices
Geography	Visits to South and Central America, Australia, Visit 23				
Bible	1 Corinthians 10, 11			Life in the Word, ch. 7, lesson 5	Life in the Word, ch. 7, lesson 5
Week 12, Lessons 116–120					
History	Exams or Catch Up or Project				
Geography	Visits to South and Central America, Australia, Visit 24				
Bible	Exams or Catch Up				

Book of Centuries Timeline

Lesson 61: More About Castles, part 5

Materials Needed

- *Castle*
- *The Magna Charta* (grades 7–9)
- *The Black Arrow* (grades 10–12)

Family: Use the illustrations in *Castle* to briefly review how far the castle has been constructed so far, then read together pages 56–61.

Grades 7–9: Read together or assign as independent reading *The Magna Charta,* Prologue and "Living in the Twelfth Century." Ask for an oral or written narration.

Grades 10–12: Assign as independent reading *The Black Arrow,* Prologue, "John Amend-All."

Lesson 62: Various History Readings

Materials Needed

- *The Sword in the Tree* (grades 1–3)
- *King Arthur and His Knights* audio recording (grades 4–6)
- *The Magna Charta* (grades 7–9)
- *Famous Men of the Middle Ages* (grades 10–12)
- *The Black Arrow* (grades 10–12)

Grades 1–3: Read together *The Sword in the Tree,* chapter 1, "Weldon Castle."

Grades 4–6: Listen with your student or assign as independent listening the audio retelling of *King Arthur and His Knights,* part 1. Ask for an oral or written narration if desired.

Grades 7–9: Read together or assign as independent reading *The Magna Charta,* "Castles and Cathedrals." Ask for an oral or written narration.

Grades 10–12: Read together or assign as independent reading *Famous Men of the Middle Ages,* chapter 23, "Peter the Hermit," and ask for a written narration. Also assign as independent reading *The Black Arrow,* Book I, chapter I, "At the Sign of the Sun in Kettley."

Reminder: *Bookmark or print the poem "The Pied Piper of Hamelin" by Robert Browning for lesson 67 for grades 4–6. You can find the poem online at http://bartleby.com or http://gutenberg.org. Also get* Adam of the Road *for lesson 70 for grades 4–6.*

Book of Centuries Timeline

Lesson 63: Visit 13 to South America & 1 Thessalonians 1 and 2

Materials Needed

- *Visits to South & Central America and Australia*
- Bible
- Envelope with heart paper inside
- Map of Paul's Journeys
- *Life in the Word* (grades 7–12)

Family Geography: Complete visit 13 in *Visits to South & Central America and Australia.*

Paul's second missionary journey (c. 49–51)

Paul writes 1 Thessalonians from Corinth (c. 49–51)

Family Bible Study: Before the lesson begins, draw a heart on a paper and put it inside an envelope. (You could alternately use a paper decorated with hearts or cut in the shape of a heart.)

Explain that on Paul's second missionary journey, he traveled to Thessalonica, a city in Macedonia that was part of the Roman Empire. Several people there listened to the gospel and believed on Jesus Christ. But trouble-makers stirred up the citizens, who worshiped the Roman gods and viewed Caesar as a god. They started a riot and forced Paul out of the city (Acts 17).

Help students locate Thessalonica on a map of "Paul's Journeys." Then help them find Corinth. Explain that a few months after Paul was forced out, he sent his friend and fellow-worker, Timothy, back to Thessalonica to see how the believers were doing. Timothy checked on that young church and then caught up with Paul at Corinth and gave his report. Overall the Thessalonian believers were doing well. However, they were a bit confused about Jesus' coming again, which He promised to do. (See John 14:3 and Acts 1:9–11.) So Paul wrote a letter to answer their questions.

Help students label an envelope to reflect this epistle to the Thessalonians: put who it was from in the return address area and to whom it was written in the middle front.

***Tip:** Don't worry about labeling this envelope as "first" at this point (for 1 Thessalonians); you will do that in lesson 78.*

Invite students to open the envelope and remove the heart paper. Explain that this epistle has a theme of "Christian love."

Read together 1 Thessalonians 1 and 2 (or divide it into smaller portions over several days: 1:1–10, 2:1–12, 2:13–20). Encourage students to listen for descriptions of how much Paul loved the believers at Thessalonica.

Focus on 1 Thessalonians 2:11 and 12. Discuss: What relationship did Paul use to picture his interaction with the Thessalonian believers? He used three words to describe his discussions with them; can you find them? Which one do you best like to hear and which would you rather avoid? Why? How does each of the three show Christian love?

Book of Centuries Timeline

Tip: Different translations will use different words, but they convey the ideas of encouraging, of motivating to action, and of teaching through personal witness.

Record student's discoveries from this passage on the heart paper, then put it back in the envelope for future lessons.

Grades 7–12: Help students to complete or assign as independent work *Life in the Word,* chapter 5, "Narrative Study of Acts 17," lesson 1.

 Lesson 64: More About Castles, part 6

Materials Needed

- *Castle*
- *The Magna Charta* (grades 7–9)
- *The Black Arrow* (grades 10–12)

Family: Use the illustrations on pages 56–61 of *Castle* to briefly review how far the castle was constructed last time, then read together pages 62–79, to finish the book.

Grades 7–9: Read together or assign as independent reading *The Magna Charta,* "The Laughable Adventure of the Irishmen's Whiskers" and "How King Richard Was Crowned and Went Upon the Third Crusade." Ask for an oral or written narration.

Grades 10–12: Assign as independent reading *The Black Arrow,* Book I, chapter II, "In the Fen."

 Lesson 65: Various History Readings

Materials Needed

- *The Sword in the Tree* (grades 1–3)
- *King Arthur and His Knights* audio recording (grades 4–6)
- *The Magna Charta* (grades 7–9)
- *Famous Men of the Middle Ages* (grades 10–12)
- *The Black Arrow* (grades 10–12)

Grades 1–3: Read together *The Sword in the Tree,* chapter 2, "Uncle Lionel."

Grades 4–6: Listen with your student or assign as independent listening the audio retelling of *King Arthur and His Knights,* part 2. Ask for an oral or written narration if desired.

Tip: The end of King Arthur and His Knights, *part 2, contains a section called "Merlin's Magic." Be sure to pre-listen to that section and determine whether you want your student to hear it.*

Book of Centuries Timeline

Grades 7–9: Read together or assign as independent reading *The Magna Charta,* "Of How John Tarried in England and of Richard's Return." Ask for an oral or written narration.

Frederick Barbarossa unites Germany (1152–1190)

Grades 10–12: Read together or assign as independent reading *Famous Men of the Middle Ages,* chapter 24, "Frederick Barbarossa," and ask for a written narration. Also assign as independent reading *The Black Arrow,* Book I, chapter III, "The Fen Ferry."

Tip: *Make sure older children are up to date with their* Discovering Doctrine *notebooks and their Book of Centuries entries.*

Lesson 66: The Great Charter

Materials Needed

- *A Castle with Many Rooms: The Story of the Middle Ages*
- *The Magna Charta* (grades 7–9)
- *The Black Arrow* (grades 10–12)

English nobles gain rights with The Magna Charta (1215)

Family: Ask students what they recall about the crusades and King Richard the Lionheart and how his brother Prince John had tried to seize the throne while he was gone. Read together *A Castle with Many Rooms: The Story of the Middle Ages,* chapter 19, "The Great Charter," and ask for an oral narration.

Grades 7–9: Read together or assign as independent reading *The Magna Charta,* "The Treasure of Chalus." Ask for an oral or written narration.

Grades 10–12: Assign as independent reading *The Black Arrow,* Book I, chapter IV, "A Greenwood Company."

Reminder: *Get* Cathedral *for lesson 76.*

Lesson 67: Various History Readings

Materials Needed

- *The Sword in the Tree* (grades 1–3)
- "The Pied Piper of Hamelin" (grades 4–6)
- *The Magna Charta* (grades 7–9)
- *Famous Men of the Middle Ages* (grades 10–12)
- *The Black Arrow* (grades 10–12)

Grades 1–3: Read together *The Sword in the Tree,* chapter 3, "The Oak Tree."

Grades 4–6: Read together or assign as independent reading the poem,

"The Pied Piper of Hamelin." Ask for an oral or written narration if desired.

Grades 7–9: Read together or assign as independent reading *The Magna Charta,* "Of How John Was Made King" and "A Great Lady." Ask for an oral or written narration.

Grades 10–12: Read together or assign as independent reading *Famous Men of the Middle Ages,* chapter 25, "Henry II and His Sons," and ask for a written narration. Also assign as independent reading *The Black Arrow,* Book I, chapter V, "Bloody as the Hunter."

Book of Centuries Timeline

Henry II and his sons rule in England (1189–1216)

Lesson 68: Visit 14 to South America & 1 Thessalonians 3 and 4

Materials Needed

- *Visits to South & Central America and Australia*
- *Material World*
- Bible
- Thessalonians envelope and heart paper
- *Life in the Word* (grades 7–12)

Family Geography: Complete visit 14 in *Visits to South & Central America and Australia.*

Family Bible Study: Display the envelope and heart paper from last time's Family Bible Study. Ask students what they recall about Paul's epistle to the Thessalonians so far. Explain that the section you will read today focuses on Paul's love for them and on the Christian love the Thessalonians had for each other.

Read together 1 Thessalonians 3 and 4 (or divide it into smaller portions over several days: 3:1–13, 4:1–12, 4:13–19). Encourage students to listen for more descriptions of Paul's love for the Thessalonians and of the Thessalonian believers' Christian love for each other.

Focus on 1 Thessalonians 4:13–18. Explain that the Thessalonians were concerned. Some of their loved ones had died ("fallen asleep") before Jesus came back. They were wondering what would happen to those loved ones at Jesus' return. What did Paul tell them? Why would those words encourage them?

Record student's discoveries from this passage on the heart paper, then put it back in the envelope for next time.

Grades 7–12: Help students to complete or assign as independent work *Life in the Word,* chapter 5, "Narrative Study of Acts 17," lesson 2.

Lesson 69: The Mongols

Materials Needed

- *A Castle with Many Rooms: The Story of the Middle Ages*

Book of Centuries Timeline

Genghis Khan unites the Mongols (1206)

- *The Magna Charta* (grades 7–9)
- *The Black Arrow* (grades 10–12)

Family: Ask students what they recall from last time's reading about the Magna Carta. Help students locate Mongolia on a world map (page 284 in *A Castle with Many Rooms*) and explain that today they will hear about what was happening in those lands about the same time as the nobles were getting their charter in England. Read together *A Castle with Many Rooms: The Story of the Middle Ages,* chapter 20, "The Mongols," and ask for an oral narration.

Grades 7–9: Read together or assign as independent reading *The Magna Charta,* "The Sheriff of Nottingham and the Men in Lincoln Green" and "Of How King John Lost His Lands Across the Water." Ask for an oral or written narration.

Grades 10–12: Assign as independent reading *The Black Arrow,* Book I, chapter VI, "To the Day's End."

 Lesson 70: Various History Readings

Materials Needed

- *The Sword in the Tree* (grades 1–3)
- *Adam of the Road* (grades 4–6)
- *The Magna Charta* (grades 7–9)
- *Famous Men of the Middle Ages* (grades 10–12)
- *The Black Arrow* (grades 10–12)

Grades 1–3: Read together *The Sword in the Tree,* chapter 4, "The Hunt."

Grades 4–6: Read together or assign as independent reading *Adam of the Road,* chapter 1, "Adam."

Grades 7–9: Read together or assign as independent reading *The Magna Charta,* "A Call to Arms" and "How the King's Purpose Was Prevented" and "Of How Langton Was Made Archbishop and How John Forbade Him the Kingdom." Ask for an oral or written narration.

Louis IX of France undertakes the Eighth Crusade; cut short by his death (1226–1270)

Grades 10–12: Read together or assign as independent reading *Famous Men of the Middle Ages,* chapter 26, "Louis IX," and ask for a written narration. Also assign as independent reading *The Black Arrow,* Book I, chapter VII, "The Hooded Face."

***Tip:** Make sure older children are up to date with their* Discovering Doctrine *notebooks and their Book of Centuries entries.*

Lesson 71: The Travels of Marco Polo

Materials Needed

- *A Castle with Many Rooms: The Story of the Middle Ages*
- *The Stuff They Left Behind: From the Days of the Middle Ages*
- *The Magna Charta* (grades 7–9)
- *The Black Arrow*, if needed (grades 10–12)

Family: Ask students what they recall from last time's reading about the Mongols and Genghis Khan. Help students locate Mongolia on a world map (page 284 in *A Castle with Many Rooms*), then see if they can find Cambodia. Display and discuss the picture of the Angkor Wat in *The Stuff They Left Behind: From the Days of the Middle Ages.* Look again at the map to see how far away Italy is from Asia and explain that in today's reading they will hear about a family who traveled from Italy to China. Read together *A Castle with Many Rooms: The Story of the Middle Ages,* chapter 21, "The Travels of Marco Polo," and ask for an oral narration.

Grades 7–9: Read together or assign as independent reading *The Magna Charta,* "The Hands of Rage and Cruelty" and "The Great Assembly at Barham Down." Ask for an oral or written narration.

Grades 10–12: Use today to catch up on any assigned reading in *The Black Arrow* if needed.

Reminder: Get In Freedom's Cause *for lesson 81 for grades 7–9.*

Book of Centuries Timeline

Marco Polo travels in the Far East; serves under Kublai Khan (1254–1324)

Lesson 72: Various History Readings

Materials Needed

- *The Sword in the Tree* (grades 1–3)
- *Adam of the Road* (grades 4–6)
- *The Magna Charta* (grades 7–9)
- *Famous Men of the Middle Ages* (grades 10–12)
- *The Black Arrow* (grades 10–12)

Grades 1–3: Read together *The Sword in the Tree,* chapter 5, "The Sword."

Grades 4–6: Read together or assign as independent reading *Adam of the Road,* the first half of chapter 2, "Nick."

Grades 7–9: Read together or assign as independent reading *The Magna Charta,* "Of How John Surrendered His Kingdom" and "Of How the King of France Was Greatly Discomfited." Ask for an oral or written narration.

Grades 10–12: Read together or assign as independent reading *Famous Men of the Middle Ages,* chapter 27, "Saint Francis and Saint Dominic," and ask

St. Dominic founds the Dominican order of friars (1170–1221)

St. Francis founds the Franciscan order of friars (1182–1226)

The pope authorizes the Dominican order to carry out the Inquisition (1233)

Book of Centuries Timeline

for a written narration. Also assign as independent reading *The Black Arrow,* Book II, chapter I, "Dick Asks Questions."

Lesson 73: Visit 15 to South America & 1 Thessalonians 5

Materials Needed

- *Visits to South & Central America and Australia*
- Bible
- Thessalonians envelope and heart paper
- *Life in the Word* (grades 7–12)

Family Geography: Complete visit 15 in Visits to *South & Central America and Australia.*

Family Bible Study: Display the envelope and heart paper from last time's Family Bible Study. Ask students what they recall about Paul's epistle to the Thessalonians so far: his love for them and their love for each other. Explain that in the section you will read today, Paul gave the believers some specific ways they could show Christian love to others who are in God's family and to those who are not.

Read together 1 Thessalonians 5 (or divide it into smaller portions over several days: verses 1–11, 12–15, 16–28). Encourage students to listen for ways the Thessalonian believers could show Christian love to others.

Focus on 1 Thessalonians 5:12–18. Discuss: Rewrite the lists as opposites to help identify actions that do not show Christian love. How can we show Christian love to those who are struggling? to those in authority over us? to those who are mean to us or offend us?

Record student's discoveries from this passage on the heart paper, then put it back in the envelope.

Grades 7–12: Help students to complete or assign as independent work *Life in the Word,* chapter 6, "Book Study of 2 Thessalonians," lesson 1.

Lesson 74: Salt, Books, and Gold

Materials Needed

- *A Castle with Many Rooms: The Story of the Middle Ages*
- *The Stuff They Left Behind: From the Days of the Middle Ages*
- *The Magna Charta* (grades 7–9)
- *The Black Arrow* (grades 10–12)

Family: Ask students what they recall from last time's reading about Marco Polo and his travels to China. Help students locate Africa on a world map (page 284 in *A Castle with Many Rooms*) and explain that today they will hear the story of a place many people think is make-believe, but it really exists.

Write "Timbuktu" on a small white board or sheet of paper for students to see. Read together *A Castle with Many Rooms: The Story of the Middle Ages,* chapter 22, "Salt, Books, and Gold." Display and discuss the picture of Sankoré Madrasah in *The Stuff They Left Behind: From the Days of the Middle Ages* when you read the section about the University of Timbuktu. Ask for an oral narration.

Grades 7–9: Read together or assign as independent reading *The Magna Charta,* "Of How the King Greatly Humbled Himself" and "How Stephen Langton Found King Henry's Charter." Ask for an oral or written narration.

Grades 10–12: Assign as independent reading *The Black Arrow,* Book II, chapter II, "The Two Oaths."

Book of Centuries Timeline

Mansa Musa establishes University of Timbuktu (c. 1327)

Lesson 75: Various History Readings

Materials Needed

- *The Sword in the Tree* (grades 1–3)
- *Adam of the Road* (grades 4–6)
- *The Magna Charta* (grades 7–9)
- *Famous Men of the Middle Ages* (grades 10–12)
- *The Black Arrow* (grades 10–12)

Grades 1–3: Read together *The Sword in the Tree,* chapter 6, "Words in the Ashes."

Grades 4–6: Read together or assign as independent reading *Adam of the Road,* the last half of chapter 2, "Nick."

Grades 7–9: Read together or assign as independent reading *The Magna Charta,* "Of How Philip Smote His Enemies & King John's Return to England" and "Of How King John Denied His Barons." Ask for an oral or written narration.

Grades 10–12: Read together or assign as independent reading *Famous Men of the Middle Ages,* chapter 28, "Marco Polo," and ask for a written narration. Also assign as independent reading *The Black Arrow,* Book II, chapter III, "The Room over the Chapel."

Tip: *Make sure older children are up to date with their* Discovering Doctrine *notebooks and their Book of Centuries entries.*

Lesson 76: Cathedral, part 1

Materials Needed

- *Cathedral*

Book of Centuries Timeline

- *The Magna Charta* (grades 7–9)
- *The Black Arrow* (grades 10–12)

Family: Ask students what they recall from last time's reading about Timbuktu and its University. Explain that today they will begin a book about a different building that was being constructed in Europe about the same time. Read together *Cathedral,* pages 5–27.

Grades 7–9: Read together or assign as independent reading *The Magna Charta,* "How John Deceitfully Gave Consent to the Charter" and "Runnymede, June 15, 1215" and "How King John Hid Himself and Laid Plots Against the Barons." Ask for an oral or written narration.

Grades 10–12: Assign as independent reading *The Black Arrow,* Book II, chapter IV, "The Passage."

Lesson 77: Various History Readings

Materials Needed

- *The Sword in the Tree* (grades 1–3)
- *Adam of the Road* (grades 4–6)
- *The Magna Charta* (grades 7–9)
- *Famous Men of the Middle Ages* (grades 10–12)
- *The Black Arrow* (grades 10–12)

Grades 1–3: Read together *The Sword in the Tree,* chapter 7, "The Robbers."

Grades 4–6: Read together or assign as independent reading *Adam of the Road,* chapter 3, "Roger."

Grades 7–9: Read together or assign as independent reading *The Magna Charta,* "The Siege of Rochester" and "Of How the Pope Rebuked the King's Enemies." Ask for an oral or written narration.

Robert Bruce leads war for independence from England; crowned king of Scotland (1306–1329)

Grades 10–12: Read together or assign as independent reading *Famous Men of the Middle Ages,* chapter 29, "Robert Bruce," and ask for a written narration. Assign as independent reading *The Black Arrow,* Book II, chapter V, "How Dick Changed Sides."

Lesson 78: Visit 16 to South America & 2 Thessalonians 1 and 2

Materials Needed

- *Visits to South & Central America and Australia*
- Bible
- Envelope and labeled paper
- *Life in the Word* (grades 7–12)

Book of Centuries Timeline

Family Geography: Complete visit 16 in *Visits to South & Central America and Australia.*

Family Bible Study: Before the lesson begins, label a paper with one red heart and two red checkmarks and put it in an envelope. Ask students what they recall about Paul's letter to the Thessalonian believers. Show them the Thessalonian envelope and heart paper that they have completed to prompt their memories.

Explain that soon after Paul sent his first letter to the believers at Thessalonica, he received word that the situation there had gone a step further. Now the teaching was going around that Jesus' second coming had already happened. Besides that problem, some of the believers had quit working and were expecting the other members of the church to feed them and take care of them. So Paul wrote another letter to the Thessalonians to reassure them about the Second Coming and to deal with the lazy believers who were refusing to earn their own living.

Paul writes 2 Thessalonians from Corinth (c. 49–51)

Help students address a new envelope (the one for this lesson) to reflect another letter to the believers at Thessalonica. Ask them to number the two envelopes to show which was the first letter and which was the second. Explain that the same numbers are used in the Bible to designate the epistles' order: 1 Thessalonians and 2 Thessalonians.

Allow a student to remove the paper with the checkmarks from the new envelope. Explain that in this second letter they will hear Paul give a reassurance of his love and two corrections. They should listen closely for the reassurance and one correction today.

Read together 2 Thessalonians 1 and 2 (or divide it into smaller portions over several days: 1:1–12; 2:1–12; 2:13–17). Ask students to narrate Paul's reassurance of his love for the Thessalonians and his first correction. Record their narrations on the paper, then put it back in the envelope for next time.

Focus on 2 Thessalonians 1:9–12. Discuss: Unbelievers were persecuting Paul's friends. What did he say would be the fate of those who do not believe the gospel of Jesus? And what was his prayer for his friends at Thessalonica? Think of a believer whom you love and pray the same things for him or her.

Grades 7–12: Help students to complete or assign as independent work *Life in the Word,* chapter 6, "Book Study of 2 Thessalonians," lesson 2.

 Lesson 79: Cathedral, part 2

Materials Needed

- *Cathedral*
- *The Magna Charta* (grades 7–9)
- *The Black Arrow*, if needed (grades 10–12)

Family: Use the illustrations on pages 6–27 in *Cathedral* to review how far construction has come so far, then read together pages 28–37.

Book of Centuries Timeline

Grades 7–9: Read together or assign as independent reading *The Magna Charta,* "Louis Invades England" and "How the Earth and the Sea Overtook the King." Ask for an oral or written narration.

Grades 10–12: Use today to catch up on any assigned reading in *The Black Arrow* if needed.

Lesson 80: Various History Readings

Materials Needed

- *The Sword in the Tree* (grades 1–3)
- *Adam of the Road* (grades 4–6)
- *The Magna Charta* (grades 7–9)
- *Famous Men of the Middle Ages* (grades 10–12)
- *The Black Arrow* (grades 10–12)

Grades 1–3: Read together *The Sword in the Tree,* chapter 8, "Magnus."

Grades 4–6: Read together or assign as independent reading *Adam of the Road,* the first half of chapter 4, "The Road."

Grades 7–9: Read together or assign as independent reading *The Magna Charta,* "How Stephen Langton Waited in Rome" and "Hubert de Burgh's Great Victory" and "The Treaty of Lambeth." Ask for an oral or written narration.

Grades 10–12: Read together or assign as independent reading *Famous Men of the Middle Ages,* chapter 30, "Edward, The Black Prince," and ask for a written narration. Also assign as independent reading *The Black Arrow,* Book III, chapter I, "The House by the Shore."

***Tip:** Make sure older children are up to date with their* Discovering Doctrine *notebooks and their Book of Centuries entries.*

Lesson 81: Cathedral, part 3

Materials Needed

- *Cathedral*
- *In Freedom's Cause* (grades 7–9)
- *The Black Arrow* (grades 10–12)

Family: Use the illustrations on pages 28–37 in *Cathedral* to review how far construction has come so far, then read together pages 38–51.

Grades 7–9: Read together or assign as independent reading *In Freedom's Cause,* chapter 1, "Glen Cairn."

Book of Centuries Timeline

Grades 10–12: Assign as independent reading *The Black Arrow,* Book III, chapter II, "A Skirmish in the Dark."

Lesson 82: Various History Readings

Materials Needed

- *The Sword in the Tree* (grades 1–3)
- *Adam of the Road* (grades 4–6)
- *In Freedom's Cause* (grades 7–9)
- *Famous Men of the Middle Ages* (grades 10–12)
- *The Black Arrow* (grades 10–12)

Grades 1–3: Read together *The Sword in the Tree,* chapter 9, "A Promise."

Grades 4–6: Read together or assign as independent reading *Adam of the Road,* the last half of chapter 4, "The Road."

Grades 7–9: Read together or assign as independent reading *In Freedom's Cause,* chapter 2, "Leaving Home."

Grades 10–12: Read together or assign as independent reading *Famous Men of the Middle Ages,* chapter 31, "William Tell and Arnold von Winkelried," and ask for a written narration. Also assign as independent reading *The Black Arrow,* Book III, chapter III, "St. Bride's Cross."

Lesson 83: Visit 17 to South America & 2 Thessalonians 3

Materials Needed

- *Visits to South & Central America and Australia*
- *Material World*
- Bible
- Envelopes and labeled papers for both Thessalonians epistles
- *Life in the Word* (grades 7–12)

Family Geography: Complete visit 17 in *Visits to South & Central America and Australia.*

Family Bible Study: Display the two Thessalonian envelopes and ask students what they recall about the two epistles. Remove the checkmark paper from the 2 Thessalonians envelope and review the reassurance and the first correction that students narrated last time. Explain that they should listen for the second correction in today's reading.

Read together 2 Thessalonians 3 (or divide it into smaller portions over several days: verses 1–5, 6–15, 16–18). Ask students to narrate Paul's second correction for the Thessalonians. Record their narrations on the paper, then put it back in the envelope.

Book of Centuries Timeline

Focus on 2 Thessalonians 3:10–12. Discuss: What is a busybody? How is that different from being busy at work? This was not the first time Paul encouraged them to work. Look back at 1 Thessalonians 4:11 and 12. Why is it important to work?

Grades 7–12: Help students to complete or assign as independent work *Life in the Word,* chapter 6, "Book Study of 2 Thessalonians," lesson 3.

 Lesson 84: Cathedral, part 4

Materials Needed
- *Cathedral*
- *The Stuff They Left Behind: From the Days of the Middle Ages*
- *In Freedom's Cause* (grades 7–9)
- *The Black Arrow* (grades 10–12)

Family: Use the illustrations on pages 38–51 in *Cathedral* to review how far construction has come so far, then read together pages 52–63. Display and discuss the picture of stained glass in *The Stuff They Left Behind: From the Days of the Middle Ages.*

Grades 7–9: Read together or assign as independent reading *In Freedom's Cause,* chapter 3, "Sir William Wallace."

Grades 10–12: Assign as independent reading *The Black Arrow,* Book III, chapter IV, "The Good Hope."

 Lesson 85: Various History Readings

Materials Needed
- *The Sword in the Tree* (grades 1–3)
- *Adam of the Road* (grades 4–6)
- *In Freedom's Cause* (grades 7–9)
- *Famous Men of the Middle Ages* (grades 10–12)
- *The Black Arrow* (grades 10–12)

Grades 1–3: Read together *The Sword in the Tree,* chapter 10, "Camelot."

Grades 4–6: Read together or assign as independent reading *Adam of the Road,* the first half of chapter 5, "Going to London."

Grades 7–9: Read together or assign as independent reading *In Freedom's Cause,* chapter 4, "The Capture of Lanark."

Tamerlane the Mongol conquers much of Asia (1333–1405)

Grades 10–12: Read together or assign as independent reading *Famous Men of the Middle Ages,* chapter 32, "Tamerlane," and ask for a written narration. Also assign as independent reading *The Black Arrow,* Book III, chapter V, "The Good Hope (continued)."

Tip: Make sure older children are up to date with their Discovering Doctrine *notebooks and their Book of Centuries entries.*

Book of Centuries Timeline

 Lesson 86: Cathedral, part 5

Materials Needed

- *Cathedral*
- *In Freedom's Cause* (grades 7–9)
- *The Black Arrow* (grades 10–12)

Family: Use the illustrations on pages 52–63 in *Cathedral* to review how far construction has come so far, then read together pages 64–79 to finish the book.

Grades 7–9: Read together or assign as independent reading *In Freedom's Cause,* chapter 5, "A Treacherous Plot."

Grades 10–12: Assign as independent reading *The Black Arrow,* Book III, chapter VI, "The Good Hope (concluded)."

 Lesson 87: Various History Readings

Materials Needed

- *The Sword in the Tree* (grades 1–3)
- *Adam of the Road* (grades 4–6)
- *In Freedom's Cause* (grades 7–9)
- *Famous Men of the Middle Ages* (grades 10–12)
- *The Black Arrow*, if needed (grades 10–12)

Grades 1–3: Read together *The Sword in the Tree,* chapter 11, "King Arthur."

Grades 4–6: Read together or assign as independent reading *Adam of the Road,* the last half of chapter 5, "Going to London."

Grades 7–9: Read together or assign as independent reading *In Freedom's Cause,* chapter 6, "The Barns of Ayr."

Grades 10–12: Read together or assign as independent reading *Famous Men of the Middle Ages,* chapter 33, "Henry V," and ask for a written narration. Also use today to catch up on any assigned reading in *The Black Arrow* if needed.

Henry V of England acquires peace treaty with France (1413–1422)

 Lesson 88: Visit 18 to South America & 1 Corinthians 1

Materials Needed

- *Visits to South & Central America and Australia*

Book of Centuries Timeline

- Bible
- Map of Paul's Journeys
- Envelope with labeled paper
- *Life in the Word* (grades 7–12)

Family Geography: Complete visit 18 in *Visits to South & Central America and Australia.*

Family Bible Study: Before the lesson begins, write "GETTING ALONG" vertically on the left side of a paper, one uppercase letter per line. Put the paper inside an envelope.

Display the four envelopes that contain the students' summaries of the four epistles studied so far this year: James, Galatians, 1 Thessalonians, 2 Thessalonians. See what the students can recall about each one.

Help students locate Corinth on a map of Paul's Journeys. Explain that Paul stopped at Corinth during his second missionary journey and stayed for more than a year, preaching the gospel and establishing the new believers in their faith in Jesus Christ. (See Acts 18.) When Paul went on to Ephesus, he sent a letter back to the Corinthian believers to encourage them to live pure lives. (We do not have a copy of that letter today, but Paul referred to it in his subsequent letters to the Corinthians that you will read.)

Paul writes 1 Corinthians from Ephesus (c. 53–55)

Soon Paul received a reply; the Corinthian believers had misunderstood some parts of his letter and were having a lot of problems. Some were living in sin; some didn't understand God's plan for marriage; some were causing divisions between people; some were disrupting the church's meetings; and some were questioning Jesus' resurrection. Paul responded by writing a lengthy letter to the Corinthians to try to set things straight and teach them how to get along as God's children. That is the letter you will read now: 1 Corinthians.

Help students address the new envelope to reflect 1 Corinthians, then show them the labeled paper you put inside it. Write "Getting Along" on the paper, using the top "G" on the paper as the first letter of your phrase. Explain that as you work your way through this epistle, the students will need to think of a phrase that summarizes each reading and, for an extra challenge, it must start with the next letter listed down the left side of the page.

Read together 1 Corinthians 1 (or divide it into smaller portions over several days: verses 1–5, 6–15, 16–18).

Focus on 1 Corinthians 1:10–13. Explain that the Corinthians were competing with each other based on who had baptized them. Today it would be similar to competing about who your pastor is or what famous person you know. Discuss: What other kinds of things do people in God's family tend to compete about? What does competition like that do to a group? How could a reminder of "by the name of our Lord Jesus Christ" help quarreling believers to get along?

Ask students to summarize the main idea of today's passage—either what the problem was or Paul's counsel to help the Corinthians get along. Tell students to make sure their summary statement begins with the letter *E*. Record their summary statement on the paper, using the *E* as the first letter.

Return the paper to the envelope for future lessons.

Grades 7–12: Help students to complete or assign as independent work *Life in the Word,* chapter 6, "Book Study of 2 Thessalonians," lesson 4.

Lesson 89: A Fresh Breeze

Materials Needed

- *A Castle with Many Rooms: The Story of the Middle Ages*
- *In Freedom's Cause* (grades 7–9)
- *The Black Arrow* (grades 10–12)

Family: Have students find France, where the cathedral they have read about was constructed, on the map on page 282 in *A Castle with Many Rooms*, Europe in the 14th Century. Then help them find Italy and the town of Florence. Explain that people living in Florence were about to make some changes that would blow like a fresh wind across Europe in the coming years. Today they will hear about the first breezes that stirred. Read together *A Castle with Many Rooms: The Story of the Middle Ages,* chapter 23, "A Fresh Breeze," and ask for an oral narration.

Book of Centuries Timeline

Giotto, first Renaissance artist (1267–1337)

Grades 7–9: Read together or assign as independent reading *In Freedom's Cause,* chapter 7, "The Cave in the Pentlands."

Grades 10–12: Assign as independent reading *The Black Arrow,* Book IV, chapter I, "The Den."

Lesson 90: Various History Readings

Materials Needed

- *The Sword in the Tree* (grades 1–3)
- *Adam of the Road* (grades 4–6)
- *In Freedom's Cause* (grades 7–9)
- *Famous Men of the Middle Ages* (grades 10–12)
- *The Black Arrow* (grades 10–12)

Grades 1–3: Read together *The Sword in the Tree,* chapter 12, "Sir Gareth."

Grades 4–6: Read together or assign as independent reading *Adam of the Road,* the first half of chapter 6, "A Blush of Boys."

Grades 7–9: Read together or assign as independent reading *In Freedom's Cause,* chapter 8, "The Council at Stirling."

Grades 10–12: Read together or assign as independent reading *Famous Men of the Middle Ages,* chapter 34, "Joan of Arc," and ask for a written narration. Also assign as independent reading *The Black Arrow,* Book IV, chapter II, "In Mine Enemies' House."

Book of Centuries Timeline

Tip: Make sure older children are up to date with their Discovering Doctrine *notebooks and their Book of Centuries entries.*

Reminder: *Get* Around the World in a Hundred Years *for lesson 99. Also get* Brother Francis and the Friendly Beasts *for lesson 100 for grades 1–3 and* Famous Men of the Renaissance and Reformation *and* Voices of the Renaissance and Reformation *for lesson 100 for grades 10–12.*

Lesson 91: Freedom Fighter

Materials Needed

- *A Castle with Many Rooms: The Story of the Middle Ages*
- *In Freedom's Cause* (grades 7–9)
- *The Black Arrow* (grades 10–12)

William Tell fights for freedom in Switzerland (c. 1273–1291)

Family: Ask students what they recall from last time's reading about the changes that were stirring in Florence, Italy. Help students find the territory of modern-day Switzerland on the map on page 282 in *A Castle with Many Rooms,* Europe in the 14th Century. Explain that while Giotto's talent as an artist was being discovered in Italy, a man with a bow and arrow in Switzerland was about to shoot an apple off his son's head. Read together *A Castle with Many Rooms: The Story of the Middle Ages,* chapter 24, "Freedom Fighter," and ask for an oral narration.

Grades 7–9: Read together or assign as independent reading *In Freedom's Cause,* chapter 9, "The Battle of Stirling Bridge."

Grades 10–12: Assign as independent reading *The Black Arrow,* Book IV, chapter III, "The Dead Spy."

Lesson 92: Various History Readings

Materials Needed

- *The Sword in the Tree* (grades 1–3)
- *Adam of the Road* (grades 4–6)
- *In Freedom's Cause* (grades 7–9)
- *Famous Men of the Middle Ages* (grades 10–12)
- *The Black Arrow* (grades 10–12)

Grades 1–3: Read together *The Sword in the Tree,* chapter 13, "The Field of Battle."

Grades 4–6: Read together or assign as independent reading *Adam of the Road,* the last half of chapter 6, "A Blush of Boys."

Grades 7–9: Read together or assign as independent reading *In Freedom's Cause,* chapter 10, "The Battle of Falkirk."

Grades 10–12: Read together or assign as independent reading *Famous Men of the Middle Ages,* chapter 35, "Warwick the Kingmaker," and ask for a written narration. Also assign as independent reading *The Black Arrow,* Book IV, chapter IV, "In the Abbey Church."

Book of Centuries Timeline

Warwick the Kingmaker ignites the thirty-year civil War of the Roses in England (1428–1471)

Lesson 93: Visit 19 to South America & 1 Corinthians 2 and 3

Materials Needed

- *Visits to South & Central America and Australia*
- Bible
- 1 Corinthians envelope and acrostic
- *Life in the Word* (grades 7–12)

Family Geography: Complete visit 19 in *Visits to South & Central America and Australia.*

Family Bible Study: Display the 1 Corinthians envelope and acrostic paper and ask students what they recall from last time's reading in this epistle. Explain that in today's reading Paul talked more about why the believers in Corinth should not be competing, boasting, and divided.

Read together 1 Corinthians 2 and 3 (or divide it into smaller portions over several days: 2:1–13, 2:14—3:9, 3:10–23).

Focus on 1 Corinthians 3:1–7. Discuss: How were the Corinthians acting like babies? Instead of viewing their favorite leaders as celebrities, how did Paul say they should view them? Who should be the famous One? How can you tell whether a person is a spiritual baby or more grown up in the Lord?

Ask students to summarize the main idea of today's passage—either what the problem was or Paul's counsel to help the Corinthians get along. Tell students to make sure their summary statement begins with the letter *T*. Record their summary statement on the paper, using the first *T* as the first letter. Return the paper to the envelope for future lessons.

Grades 7–12: Help students to complete or assign as independent work *Life in the Word,* chapter 7, "Character Study on Paul," lesson 1.

Lesson 94: The Black Prince, the Black Death, and the White Knight of Orleans

Materials Needed

- *A Castle with Many Rooms: The Story of the Middle Ages*
- *In Freedom's Cause* (grades 7–9)
- *The Black Arrow* (grades 10–12)

Book of Centuries Timeline

Hundred Years War between France and England (1337–1453)

Black Death comes to Europe; kills one-third its population (1347–1350)

Joan of Arc leads France to victory (1412–1431)

Family: Ask students what they recall from last time's reading about William Tell and the fight for freedom in Switzerland. Explain that while Switzerland was fighting for its freedom, England and France started a quarrel that would last for 100 years. Read together *A Castle with Many Rooms: The Story of the Middle Ages,* chapter 25, "The Black Prince, the Black Death, and the White Knight of Orleans." Use the map on page 282, Europe in the 14th Century, to help students follow the story. Ask for an oral narration.

Grades 7–9: Read together or assign as independent reading *In Freedom's Cause,* chapter 11, "Robert the Bruce."

Grades 10–12: Assign as independent reading *The Black Arrow,* Book IV, chapter V, "Earl Risingham."

 Lesson 95: Various History Readings

Materials Needed

- *The Sword in the Tree* (grades 1–3)
- *Adam of the Road* (grades 4–6)
- *In Freedom's Cause* (grades 7–9)
- *Famous Men of the Middle Ages* (grades 10–12)
- *The Black Arrow* (grades 10–12)

Grades 1–3: Read together *The Sword in the Tree,* chapter 14, "The Dungeon."

Grades 4–6: Read together or assign as independent reading *Adam of the Road,* the first half of chapter 7, "Jankin."

Grades 7–9: Read together or assign as independent reading *In Freedom's Cause,* chapter 12, "The Battle of Methven."

Grades 10–12: Read together or assign as independent reading *Famous Men of the Middle Ages,* chapter 36, "Gutenberg," and ask for a written narration. Also assign as independent reading *The Black Arrow,* Book IV, chapter VI, "Arblaster Again."

***Tip:** Make sure older children are up to date with their* Discovering Doctrine *notebooks and their Book of Centuries entries.*

 Lesson 96: Conquerors of the Green Sea

Materials Needed

- *A Castle with Many Rooms: The Story of the Middle Ages*
- *In Freedom's Cause* (grades 7–9)
- *The Black Arrow* (grades 10–12)

Family: Ask students what they recall from last time's reading about the Hundred Years War between France and England. Explain that while England and France were busy fighting each other, others set out to explore more of the world. Read together *A Castle with Many Rooms: The Story of the Middle Ages,* chapter 26, "Conquerors of the Green Sea." Use a world map (page 284) to help students find Portugal and trace the explorations. Ask for an oral narration.

Grades 7–9: Read together or assign as independent reading *In Freedom's Cause,* chapter 13, "The Castle of Dunstaffnage."

Grades 10–12: Assign as independent reading *The Black Arrow,* Book V, chapter I, "The Shrill Trumpet."

Book of Centuries Timeline

Prince Henry the Navigator begins the Age of Exploration (1421–1460)

Lesson 97: Various History Readings

Materials Needed

- *The Sword in the Tree,* if needed (grades 1–3)
- *Adam of the Road* (grades 4–6)
- *In Freedom's Cause* (grades 7–9)
- *Famous Men of the Middle Ages,* if needed (grades 10–12)
- *The Black Arrow* (grades 10–12)

Grades 1–3: Use today to catch up and finish reading *The Sword in the Tree* as needed.

Grades 4–6: Read together or assign as independent reading *Adam of the Road,* the last half of chapter 7, "Jankin."

Grades 7–9: Read together or assign as independent reading *In Freedom's Cause,* chapter 14, "Colonsay."

Grades 10–12: Use today to catch up and finish *Famous Men of the Middle Ages* if needed. Also assign as independent reading *The Black Arrow,* Book V, chapter II, "The Battle of Shoreby."

Lesson 98: Visit 20 to South America & 1 Corinthians 4 and 5

Materials Needed

- *Visits to South & Central America and Australia*
- Bible
- 1 Corinthians envelope and acrostic
- *Life in the Word* (grades 7–12)

Family Geography: Complete visit 20 in *Visits to South & Central America and Australia.*

Book of Centuries Timeline

Family Bible Study: Display the 1 Corinthians envelope and acrostic paper and ask students what they recall about this epistle so far. Explain that in today's reading Paul reminded the believers that pride and boasting have no place in ministry, and especially not when it concerns sin.

Read together 1 Corinthians 4 and 5 (or divide it into smaller portions over several days: 4:1–7, 4:8–21, 5:1–8, 5:9–13).

Focus on 1 Corinthians 5:6–8. Discuss: What is leaven? How does a little leaven affect a whole loaf of bread? How does one person's attitude or action affect a whole family or group?

Ask students to summarize the main idea of today's passage—either what the problem was or Paul's counsel to help the Corinthians get along. Tell students to make sure their summary statement begins with the letter *T*. Record their summary statement on the paper, using the remaining *T* as the first letter. Return the paper to the envelope for future lessons.

Grades 7–12: Help students to complete or assign as independent work *Life in the Word,* chapter 7, "Character Study on Paul," lesson 2.

Lesson 99: Bartholomew Diaz

Materials Needed

- *Around the World in a Hundred Years*
- *In Freedom's Cause* (grades 7–9)
- *The Black Arrow* (grades 10–12)

Family: Write "Age of Exploration" on a small white board or sheet of paper. Discuss what it means and what part Prince Henry played in starting it. Explain that you're going to read about more explorers who picked up where Prince Henry left off. Write "Bartholomew Diaz" on the white board and explain that today's reading will be about this man's explorations. Read together *Around the World in a Hundred Years,* chapter 3, "Bartholomew Diaz." Use the map on page 30 of that book to help students trace Diaz's explorations. Ask for an oral narration.

Bartholomew Diaz explores Africa's coastline to the Cape of Good Hope (1487–1500)

Tip: *The material in chapters 1 and 2 were already covered in* A Castle with Many Rooms, *chapter 26, so we will pick up the explorations with chapter 3.*

Grades 7–9: Read together or assign as independent reading *In Freedom's Cause,* chapter 15, "A Mission to Ireland."

Grades 10–12: Assign as independent reading *The Black Arrow,* Book V, chapter III, "The Battle of Shoreby (concluded)."

Lesson 100: Various History Readings

Materials Needed

- *Brother Francis and the Friendly Beasts* (grades 1–3)

- *Adam of the Road* (grades 4–6)
- *In Freedom's Cause* (grades 7–9)
- *Famous Men of the Renaissance and Reformation* (grades 10–12)
- *Voices of the Renaissance and Reformation* (grades 10–12)

Grades 1–3: Read together *Brother Francis and the Friendly Beasts,* the first five pages of text, from "In the old Italian town of Assisi" to "They called themselves brothers as they went, two by two, preaching and helping the poor."

Grades 4–6: Read together or assign as independent reading *Adam of the Road,* the first half of chapter 8, "Red in the Morning."

Grades 7–9: Read together or assign as independent reading *In Freedom's Cause,* chapter 16, "An Irish Rising."

Grades 10–12: Read together or assign as independent reading *Famous Men of the Renaissance and Reformation,* chapter 1, "Petrarch," and ask for a written narration. Also assign Petrarch's autobiography and sonnets in *Voices of the Renaissance and Reformation,* pages 3–12.

> ***Tip:*** *Make sure older children are up to date with their* Discovering Doctrine *notebooks and their Book of Centuries entries.*

Book of Centuries Timeline

Petrarch begins to revive interest in classical Greek and Roman ideas (1304–1374)

 Lesson 101: Christopher Columbus

Materials Needed

- *Around the World in a Hundred Years*
- *The Stuff They Left Behind: From the Days of the Middle Ages*
- *In Freedom's Cause* (grades 7–9)
- *The Black Arrow* (grades 10–12)

Family: Ask students what they recall from last time's reading about Bartholomew Diaz and the Cape of Good Hope. Explain that today's reading is about one of the most famous explorers who lived in that time: Christopher Columbus. Read together *Around the World in a Hundred Years,* chapter 4, "Christopher Columbus." Use the map on page 38 of that book to help students trace Columbus' voyages. Ask for an oral narration, then display and discuss the picture of Alhambra in *The Stuff They Left Behind: From the Days of the Middle Ages.*

Christopher Columbus discovers islands off the Americas' coast, looking for Asia (1492–1504)

> ***Tip:*** *The author of* Around the World in a Hundred Years *does not write from a Christian worldview. You may be able to use some of her comments in the text as discussion starters with your older students.*

Grades 7–9: Read together or assign as independent reading *In Freedom's*

Book of Centuries Timeline

Cause, chapter 17, "The King's Blood-Hound."

Grades 10–12: Assign as independent reading *The Black Arrow,* Book V, chapter IV, "The Sack of Shoreby."

 Lesson 102: Various History Readings

Materials Needed

- *Brother Francis and the Friendly Beasts* (grades 1–3)
- *Adam of the Road* (grades 4–6)
- *In Freedom's Cause* (grades 7–9)
- *Famous Men of the Renaissance and Reformation* (grades 10–12)
- *The Black Arrow* (grades 10–12)

Grades 1–3: Read together *Brother Francis and the Friendly Beasts,* the next four pages of text, from "Francis preached to animals" through "Francis would carry him home as a good shepherd carries a lamb."

Grades 4–6: Read together or assign as independent reading *Adam of the Road,* the last half of chapter 8, "Red in the Morning."

Grades 7–9: Read together or assign as independent reading *In Freedom's Cause,* chapter 18, "The Hound Restored."

Grades 10–12: Read together or assign as independent reading *Famous Men of the Renaissance and Reformation,* chapter 2, "Giotto," and ask for a written narration. Also assign as independent reading *The Black Arrow,* Book V, chapter V, "Night in the Woods: Alicia Risingham."

Reminder: *Get* A Medieval Feast *for lesson 112 for grades 1–3.*

 Lesson 103: Visit 21 to South America & 1 Corinthians 6 and 7

Materials Needed

- *Visits to South & Central America and Australia*
- *Hungry Planet: What the World Eats*
- Bible
- 1 Corinthians envelope and acrostic
- *Life in the Word* (grades 7–12)

Family Geography: Complete visit 21 in *Visits to South & Central America and Australia.*

Family Bible Study: Display the 1 Corinthians envelope and acrostic paper and ask students what they recall about this epistle so far. Explain that in today's reading Paul addressed the topics of getting along well in personal conflicts and in marriage situations.

Read together 1 Corinthians 6 and 7 (or divide it into smaller portions over several days: 6:1–11, 6:12–20, 7:1–16, 7:17–24, 7:25–40).

Focus on 1 Corinthians 6:12. Discuss: Sometimes we feel like we can do anything we want to as long as it's not against the law or there isn't a definite rule that says we can't. But this verse gives two other tests to help us determine whether to do something. What are they? How can those two guidelines help us make wise choices? How can they help us get along with others?

***Tip:** The phrase "all things are lawful for me" is most likely a popular saying that the Corinthians were using to justify their satisfying their physical lusts.*

Ask students to summarize a main idea from today's passage—either what the problem was or Paul's counsel to help the Corinthians get along. Tell students to make sure their summary statement begins with the letter *I*. Record their summary statement on the paper, using the *I* as the first letter. Return the paper to the envelope for future lessons.

Grades 7–12: Help students to complete or assign as independent work *Life in the Word,* chapter 7, "Character Study on Paul," lesson 3.

Book of Centuries Timeline

 Lesson 104: Vasco da Gama

Materials Needed
- *Around the World in a Hundred Years*
- *In Freedom's Cause* (grades 7–9)
- *The Black Arrow* (grades 10–12)

Family: Ask students what they recall from last time's reading about Christopher Columbus. Explain that his explorations prompted Spain to do more exploring too. Write "Vasco da Gama" on the white board and explain that today's reading will be about this man's explorations. Read together *Around the World in a Hundred Years,* chapter 5, "Vasco da Gama." Use the map on page 50 of that book to help students trace da Gama's explorations. Ask for an oral narration.

Vasco da Gama sails around Africa to India (1497–1502)

Grades 7–9: Read together or assign as independent reading *In Freedom's Cause,* chapter 19, "The Convent of St. Kenneth."

Grades 10–12: Assign as independent reading *The Black Arrow,* Book V, chapter VI, "Night in the Woods (concluded): Dick and Joan."

Book of Centuries Timeline

Lesson 105: Various History Readings

Materials Needed

- *Brother Francis and the Friendly Beasts* (grades 1–3)
- *Adam of the Road* (grades 4–6)
- *In Freedom's Cause* (grades 7–9)
- *Famous Men of the Renaissance and Reformation* (grades 10–12)
- *The Black Arrow* (grades 10–12)

Grades 1–3: Read together *Brother Francis and the Friendly Beasts,* the next four pages of text, from "One evening not long before Christmas" through "and the little town of Greccio slept under the stars."

Grades 4–6: Read together or assign as independent reading *Adam of the Road,* the first half of chapter 9, "Night in Westhumble Lane."

Grades 7–9: Read together or assign as independent reading *In Freedom's Cause,* chapter 20, "The Heiress of the Kerrs."

Filippo Brunelleschi designs dome for cathedral in Florence, Italy (1377–1446)

Donatello, sculptor and friend of Brunelleschi (1386–1466)

Grades 10–12: Read together or assign as independent reading *Famous Men of the Renaissance and Reformation,* chapter 3, "Filippo Brunelleschi and Donatello," and ask for a written narration. Also assign as independent reading *The Black Arrow,* Book V, chapter VII, "Dick's Revenge."

Tip: Make sure older children are up to date with their Discovering Doctrine *notebooks and their Book of Centuries entries.*

Lesson 106: Pedro Alvares Cabral

Materials Needed

- *Around the World in a Hundred Years*
- *In Freedom's Cause* (grades 7–9)
- *The Black Arrow* (grades 10–12)

Pedro Alvares Cabral sails to Brazil for Portugal (1500–1501)

Family: Ask students what they recall from last time's reading about Vasco da Gama. Explain that the next explorer Spain sent out could use the knowledge that Diaz and da Gama had acquired in their journeys. Write "Padro Alvares Cabral" on the white board and read together *Around the World in a Hundred Years,* chapter 6, "Pedro Alvares Cabral." Use the map on page 58 of that book to help students trace Cabral's explorations. Ask for an oral narration.

Grades 7–9: Read together or assign as independent reading *In Freedom's Cause,* chapter 21, "The Siege of Aberfilly."

Grades 10–12: Assign as independent reading *The Black Arrow,* Book V, chapter VIII, "Conclusion."

Lesson 107: Various History Readings

Materials Needed

- *Brother Francis and the Friendly Beasts* (grades 1–3)
- *Adam of the Road* (grades 4–6)
- *In Freedom's Cause* (grades 7–9)
- *Famous Men of the Renaissance and Reformation* (grades 10–12)
- *Voices of the Renaissance and Reformation* (grades 10–12)
- *The Black Arrow*, if needed (grades 10–12)

Grades 1–3: Read together *Brother Francis and the Friendly Beasts,* the last page of text that gives his song.

Grades 4–6: Read together or assign as independent reading *Adam of the Road,* the last half of chapter 9, "Night in Westhumble Lane."

Grades 7–9: Read together or assign as independent reading *In Freedom's Cause,* chapter 22, "A Prisoner."

Grades 10–12: Read together or assign as independent reading *Famous Men of the Renaissance and Reformation,* chapter 4, "Lorenzo Valla," and ask for a written narration. Also assign the excerpt from "The Donation of Constantine" in *Voices of the Renaissance and Reformation,* page 13. Use today and the rest of this term to catch up and finish *The Black Arrow* if needed.

Book of Centuries Timeline

Lorenzo Valla exposes "The Donation of Constantine" as a fraud (1407–1457)

Lesson 108: Visit 22 to South America & 1 Corinthians 8 and 9

Materials Needed

- *Visits to South & Central America and Australia*
- Bible
- 1 Corinthians envelope and acrostic
- *Life in the Word* (grades 7–12)

Family Geography: Complete visit 22 in *Visits to South & Central America and Australia.*

Family Bible Study: Display the 1 Corinthians envelope and acrostic paper and ask students what they recall about this epistle so far. Explain that in today's reading Paul encouraged the Corinthian believers to give up their rights willingly in order to help each other, just as he had given up his rights in order to help them.

Read together 1 Corinthians 8 and 9 (or divide it into smaller portions over several days: 8:1–13, 9:1–12, 9:13–23, 9:24–27).

***Tip:** Only part of the animal was used in a sacrifice to a pagan god; the rest could be eaten. So pagan temples often served as meat markets and banquet facilities.*

Book of Centuries Timeline

Focus on 1 Corinthians 9:24–27. Discuss: What do serious athletes go through in order to win the prize? How do they exercise self-discipline for the cause? What part does physical self-discipline play in God's family?

Ask students to summarize the main idea of today's passage—either what the problem was or Paul's counsel to help the Corinthians get along. Tell students to make sure their summary statement begins with the letter *N*. Record their summary statement on the paper, using the *N* as the first letter. Return the paper to the envelope for future lessons.

Grades 7–12: Help students to complete or assign as independent work *Life in the Word,* chapter 7, "Character Study on Paul," lesson 4.

 Lesson 109: John Cabot

Materials Needed

- *Around the World in a Hundred Years*
- *In Freedom's Cause* (grades 7–9)

John Cabot sails from England to Newfoundland (1497–1498)

Family: Ask students what they recall from last time's reading about Cabral. Explain that today you will read about an explorer who set out from England. Write "John Cabot" on the white board and read together *Around the World in a Hundred Years,* chapter 7, "John Cabot." Use the map on page 62 of that book to help students trace Cabot's explorations. Ask for an oral narration.

Grades 7–9: Read together or assign as independent reading *In Freedom's Cause,* chapter 23, "The Escape from Berwick."

 Lesson 110: Various History Readings

Materials Needed

- *Brother Francis and the Friendly Beasts,* if needed (grades 1–3)
- *Adam of the Road* (grades 4–6)
- *In Freedom's Cause* (grades 7–9)
- *Famous Men of the Renaissance and Reformation* (grades 10–12)

Grades 1–3: Use today to catch up and finish reading *Brother Francis and the Friendly Beasts* as needed.

Grades 4–6: Read together or assign as independent reading *Adam of the Road,* the first half of chapter 10, "Here, Nick!"

Grades 7–9: Read together or assign as independent reading *In Freedom's Cause,* chapter 24, "The Progress of the War."

Cosimo de'Medici becomes ruler of Florence, Italy (1389–1464)

Grades 10–12: Read together or assign as independent reading *Famous Men of the Renaissance and Reformation,* chapter 5, "Cosimo de' Medici," and ask for a written narration.

Tip: Make sure older children are up to date with their Discovering Doctrine *notebooks and their Book of Centuries entries.*

Reminder: *If you want to do a hands-on project for lessons 116–120, gather any supplies you might need.*

Reminder: *Start gathering the resources you will need for Term 3.* *See page 91.*

Book of Centuries Timeline

 Lesson 111: Amerigo Vespucci

Materials Needed

- *Around the World in a Hundred Years*
- *The Stuff They Left Behind: From the Days of the Middle Ages*
- *In Freedom's Cause* (grades 7–9)

Family: Show students the first two-page map at the front of *Around the World in a Hundred Years* (pages 4 and 5). Ask students to tell you what they can recall about each explorer listed there. Explain that today you will read about the one explorer on that map of whom they have not yet read. Write "Amerigo Vespucci" on the white board and read together *Around the World in a Hundred Years,* chapter 8, "Amerigo Vespucci." Use the map on page 68 of that book to help students trace Vespucci's explorations. Ask for an oral narration. Display and discuss the picture of Machu Picchu in *The Stuff They Left Behind: From the Days of the Middle Ages.*

Amerigo Vespucci gives his name to the Americas (1499–1501)

Grades 7–9: Read together or assign as independent reading *In Freedom's Cause,* chapter 25, "The Capture of a Stronghold."

 Lesson 112: Various History Readings

Materials Needed

- *Medieval Feast* (grades 1–3)
- *Adam of the Road* (grades 4–6)
- *In Freedom's Cause* (grades 7–9)
- *Famous Men of the Renaissance and Reformation* (grades 10–12)
- *Voices of the Renaissance and Reformation* (grades 10–12)

Grades 1–3: Read together *Medieval Feast.*

Grades 4–6: Read together or assign as independent reading *Adam of the Road,* the last half of chapter 10, "Here, Nick!"

Grades 7–9: Read together or assign as independent reading *In Freedom's Cause,* chapter 26, "Edinburgh."

Book of Centuries Timeline

Lorenzo de'Medici rules Florence, Italy, after his father, patrons the arts (1407–1457)

Grades 10–12: Read together or assign as independent reading *Famous Men of the Renaissance and Reformation,* chapter 6, "Lorenzo de' Medici," and ask for a written narration. Also assign Lorenzo's letter to his son Giovanni in *Voices of the Renaissance and Reformation,* pages 15–17.

Lesson 113: Visit 23 to South America & 1 Corinthians 10 and 11

Materials Needed

- *Visits to South & Central America and Australia*
- Bible
- 1 Corinthians envelope and acrostic
- *Life in the Word* (grades 7–12)

Family Geography: Complete visit 23 in *Visits to South & Central America and Australia.*

Family Bible Study: Display the 1 Corinthians envelope and acrostic paper and ask students what they recall about this epistle so far. Explain that in today's reading Paul finished his thoughts on eating food offered to idols then addressed some issues that were causing division in their worshiping together.

Read together 1 Corinthians 10 and 11 (or divide it into smaller portions over several days: 10:1–13, 10:14–33, 11:1–16, 11:17–34).

Focus on 1 Corinthians 10:13. Discuss: Finish these sentences.

"Every time I am tempted to sin, I know that . . . ."

"Because God is faithful, in the midst of my temptation I can depend on . . . ."

"When I think that I have no choice but to sin, ..."

Ask students to summarize a main idea from today's passage—either what the problem was or Paul's counsel to help the Corinthians get along. Tell students to make sure their summary statement begins with the letter *G*. Record their summary statement on the paper, using the *G* as the first letter. Return the paper to the envelope for future lessons.

Grades 7–12: Help students to complete or assign as independent work *Life in the Word,* chapter 7, "Character Study on Paul," lesson 5.

Lesson 114: Juan Ponce de Leon

Materials Needed

- *Around the World in a Hundred Years*
- *In Freedom's Cause* (grades 7–9)
- *Famous Men of the Renaissance and Reformation,* if needed (grades 10–12)
- *Voices of the Renaissance and Reformation,* if needed (grades 10–12)

Family: Ask students what they recall from last time's reading about Amerigo Vespucci. Explain that today you will read about an explorer who crossed the sea with Columbus and then explored more of his surroundings in the New World. Write "Juan Ponce de Leon" on the white board and read together *Around the World in a Hundred Years,* chapter 9, "Juan Ponce de Leon." Use the map on page 76 of that book to help students trace Ponce de Leon's explorations. Ask for an oral narration.

Tip: You will finish reading Around the World in a Hundred Years *next term.*

Grades 7–9: Read together or assign as independent reading *In Freedom's Cause,* chapter 27, "Bannockburn."

Grades 10–12: Use today to catch up on any assigned reading in *Famous Men of the Renaissance and Reformation* or *Voices of the Renaissance and Reformation* if needed.

Book of Centuries Timeline

Juan Ponce de Leon discovers Florida (1513)

 Lesson 115: Various History Readings

Materials Needed

- *Adam of the Road* (grades 4–6)
- *In Freedom's Cause*, if needed (grades 7–9)
- *Famous Men of the Renaissance and Reformation* (grades 10–12)
- *Voices of the Renaissance and Reformation* (grades 10–12)

Grades 1–3: Use today to catch up and finish any reading from this term as needed.

Grades 4–6: Read together or assign as independent reading *Adam of the Road,* chapter 11, "Adam Swims the Wey."

Grades 7–9: Use today to catch up and finish reading *In Freedom's Cause* if needed.

Grades 10–12: Read together or assign as independent reading *Famous Men of the Renaissance and Reformation,* chapter 7, "Girolamo Savonarola," and ask for a written narration. Also assign excerpts from his sermons in *Voices of the Renaissance and Reformation,* pages 19–21.

Girolamo Savonarola, Dominican preacher and evangelist, opposes the Medici family (1452–1498)

Tip: Make sure older children are up to date with their Discovering Doctrine *notebooks and their Book of Centuries entries.*

Book of Centuries Timeline

Lesson 116: History Catch Up, Exam, or Project

Materials Needed

- (optional) Materials for hands-on project

Family: Use today to catch up on any history reading you need to finish, or use the questions below for the students' exam on Middle Ages history studied so far. You may also use the history lessons this week to do an optional hands-on project if you would prefer.
Grades 1–3: Choose one of these titles and tell the story: Marco Polo Travels to China; Genghis Khan Rules on Horseback; William Tell Shoots the Arrow.
Grades 4–6: Describe how a cathedral was designed and constructed.
Grades 7–9: Tell in detail the circumstances surrounding the Magna Charta and why it is considered a significant historic document.
Grades 10–12: Describe the relationship between the church and government during the Middle Ages. Cite examples from your readings.

Optional Hands-On Project: Select a hands-on project from the Links and Tips page at http://simplycm.com/middle-ages-links.

Lesson 117: History Catch Up, Exam, or Project

Materials Needed

- (optional) Materials for hands-on project

Family: Use today to catch up on any history reading you need to finish, or use the questions below for the students' exam on Middle Ages history studied so far. You may also do an optional hands-on project.
Grades 1–3: Tell the story of an explorer you have read about this term.
Grades 4–6: Tell the story of Marco Polo.
Grades 7–9: Tell the story of Wallace and Bruce and Scotland's fight for independence.
Grades 10–12: Tell in detail about the Renaissance, including (a) what factors led up to it, (b) key people and ideas that sparked it, and (c) why and how it began to spread across Europe.

Optional Hands-On Project: Continue your selected hands-on project or start a new one if desired.

Lesson 118: Visit 24 to South America & Bible Exam

Materials Needed

- *Visits to South & Central America and Australia*

Family Geography: Complete visit 24 in *Visits to South & Central America and Australia.*

Family Bible Exam: Use today to catch up on any Bible reading you need to finish, or use the questions below for the students' exam on the epistles studied so far.
Family: Tell what you know about the two epistles that Paul wrote to the Thessalonians. And/or tell what counsel Paul gave to the Corinthians so far in his epistle to help them get along as God's children.

Tip: *It is up to you whether to ask your students to do one or both narration prompts given.*

Grades 7–12: Write (a) a summary of the book of 2 Thessalonians, chapter by chapter, and (b) a description of your findings for the character study of Paul.

Lesson 119: History Catch Up, Exam, or Project

Materials Needed
- (optional) Materials for hands-on project

Family: Use today to catch up on any history reading you need to finish, or use the questions below for the students' exam on Middle Ages history studied so far. You may also do an optional hands-on project.
Grades 1–3: Tell the story of a hero you have read about this term.
Grades 4-6: Explain how Giotto's art was different and how it helped start the Renaissance.
Grades 7-9: Choose four of the following explorers and summarize what each did to help reveal the Unknown: Prince Henry, Bartholomew Diaz, Christopher Columbus, Vasco da Gama, Pedro Alvares Cabral, John Cabot, Amerigo Vespucci, Juan Ponce de Leon.
Grades 10–12: Survey Savonarola's character and actions. Which traits are admirable and should be imitated and which are the opposite? Cite examples from the biography and sermon excerpts that you read.

Optional Hands-On Project: Continue your selected hands-on project or start a new one if desired.

Lesson 120: History Catch Up, Exam, or Project

Materials Needed
- (optional) Materials for hands-on project

Book of Centuries Timeline

Book of Centuries Timeline

Family: Use today to catch up on any history reading you need to finish, or use the questions below for the students' exam on Middle Ages history studied so far. You may also do an optional hands-on project.
Grades 1–3: Tell about a building you have learned about this term.
Grades 4–6: Tell the story of Prince Henry and the Green Sea of Darkness.
Grades 7–9: Choose one of the titles listed and write a poem that tells the Medieval event it relates to: (a) The Apple and the Arrow; (b) The Black Death; (c) The Green Sea of Darkness.
Grades 10–12: Expand your sketch or essay from last term to include the people and events listed below. Be sure to locate them in their proper geographical regions: (a) Genghis Khan, (b) Marco Polo, (c) University of Timbuktu, (d) Giotto, (e) William Tell, (f) Joan of Arc, (g) Prince Henry.

Optional Hands-On Project: Finish your selected hands-on project.

Term 3

(12 weeks; 5 lessons/week)

Term 3 Book List

Family

- *Around the World in a Hundred Years* by Jean Fritz
- Bible
- *The Bible Smuggler* by Louise Vernon
- *A Castle with Many Rooms: The Story of the Middle Ages* by Lorene Lambert
- *Material World* **and** *Hungry Planet: What the World Eats* by Peter Menzel
- *The Stuff They Left Behind: From the Days of the Middle Ages* portfolio
- *Visits to South & Central America and Australia* notebook by Sonya Shafer (one for each student)

Plus . . .

Grades 1–3

- *Castle Diary: The Journal of Tobias Burgess* by Richard Platt
- *Marguerite Makes a Book* by Bruce Robertson
- *Pippo the Fool* by Tracey E. Fern

Grades 4–6

- *Adam of the Road* by Elizabeth Janet Gray

Grades 7–9

- Book of Centuries (one for each student)
- *Discovering Doctrine* by Sonya Shafer (one for each student)
- *Life in the Word* by Sonya Shafer (one for each student)
- *The Prince and the Pauper* by Samuel Clemens (Mark Twain)

Grades 10–12

- Book of Centuries (one for each student)
- *Discovering Doctrine* by Sonya Shafer (one for each student)
- *Famous Men of the Renaissance and Reformation* by Rob Shearer
- *The King's Fifth* by Scott O'Dell
- *Life in the Word* by Sonya Shafer (one for each student)
- *The Second Mrs. Giaconda* by E. L. Konigsburg
- *Voices of the Renaissance and Reformation* by Rob Shearer

What You Will Cover As a Family

History: *From the Renaissance through the beginning of the Reformation (1469–1550)*

Geography: *Medieval Europe: Central America and the Caribbean*

Bible: *The rest of 1 Corinthians and the epistle of 2 Corinthians*

Term 3 At a Glance

	Family	Grades 1–3	Grades 4–6	Grades 7–9	Grades 10–12
			Week 1, Lessons 121–125		
History	Around the World in 100 Years, ch. 10, 11A	Marguerite Makes a Book, parts 1, 2	Adam of the Road, ch. 12	The Prince and the Pauper, ch. 1–4	Famous Men of the Ren and Ref, ch. 8, 9; Voices; The Second Mrs. Giaconda
Geography	Visits to South and Central America, Australia, Visit 25				
Bible	1 Corinthians 12, 13			Life in the Word, ch. 8, lesson 1	Life in the Word, ch. 8, lesson 1
			Week 2, Lessons 126–130		
History	Around the World in 100 Years, ch. 11B, 12	Marguerite Makes a Book, parts 3, 4	Adam of the Road, ch. 13	The Prince and the Pauper, ch. 5–7	Famous Men of the Ren and Ref, ch. 10, 11; Voices; The Second Mrs. Giaconda
Geography	Visits to South and Central America, Australia, Visit 26				
Bible	1 Corinthians 14			Life in the Word, ch. 8, lesson 2	Life in the Word, ch. 8, lesson 2
			Week 3, Lessons 131–135		
History	A Castle with Many Rooms, ch. 27, 28	Castle Diary	Adam of the Road, ch. 14	The Prince and the Pauper, ch. 8–11	Famous Men of the Ren and Ref, ch. 12, 13; Voices; The Second Mrs. Giaconda; The King's Fifth
Geography	Visits to South and Central America, Australia, Visit 27				
Bible	1 Corinthians 15			Life in the Word, ch. 9, lesson 1	Life in the Word, ch. 9, lesson 1
			Week 4, Lessons 136–140		
History	A Castle with Many Rooms, ch. 29, 30	Castle Diary	Adam of the Road, ch. 15	The Prince and the Pauper, ch. 12, 13	Famous Men of the Ren and Ref, ch. 14, 15; Voices; The King's Fifth
Geography	Visits to South and Central America, Australia, Visit 28				
Bible	1 Corinthians 16			Life in the Word, ch. 9, lesson 2	Life in the Word, ch. 9, lesson 2
			Week 5, Lessons 141–145		
History	The Bible Smuggler, ch. 1, 2	Castle Diary	Adam of the Road, ch. 16, 17A	The Prince and the Pauper, ch. 14, 15	Famous Men of the Ren and Ref, ch. 16, 17; Voices; The King's Fifth
Geography	Visits to South and Central America, Australia, Visit 29				
Bible	2 Corinthians 1, 2			Life in the Word, ch. 9, lesson 3	Life in the Word, ch. 9, lesson 3
			Week 6, Lessons 146–150		
History	The Bible Smuggler, ch. 3, 4	Castle Diary	Adam of the Road, ch. 17B, 18A	The Prince and the Pauper, ch. 16–18	Famous Men of the Ren and Ref, ch. 18, 19; Voices; The King's Fifth
Geography	Visits to South and Central America, Australia, Visit 30				
Bible	2 Corinthians 3, 4			Life in the Word, ch. 10, lesson 1	Life in the Word, ch. 10, lesson 1

Use this chart to see what your family and each of your students will be studying week by week during this term. You will also be able to see when each book is scheduled to be used.

	Family	Grades 1–3	Grades 4–6	Grades 7–9	Grades 10–12
			Week 7, Lessons 151–155		
History	The Bible Smuggler, ch. 5, 6	Castle Diary	Adam of the Road, ch. 18B, 19A	The Prince and the Pauper, ch. 19–21	Famous Men of the Ren and Ref, ch. 20, 21; Voices; The King's Fifth
Geography	Visits to South and Central America, Australia, Visit 31				
Bible	2 Corinthians 5, 6			Life in the Word, ch. 10, lesson 2	Life in the Word, ch. 10, lesson 2
			Week 8, Lessons 156–160		
History	The Bible Smuggler, ch. 7, 8	Castle Diary	Adam of the Road, ch. 19B, 20A	The Prince and the Pauper, ch. 22–25	Famous Men of the Ren and Ref, ch. 22, 23; Voices; The King's Fifth
Geography	Visits to South and Central America, Australia, Visit 32				
Bible	2 Corinthians 7, 8			Life in the Word, ch. 10, lesson 3	Life in the Word, ch. 10, lesson 3
			Week 9, Lessons 161–165		
History	The Bible Smuggler, ch. 9, 10	Castle Diary	Adam of the Road, ch. 20B, 21A	The Prince and the Pauper, ch. 26–28	Famous Men of the Ren and Ref, ch. 24, 25; Voices; The King's Fifth
Geography	Visits to South and Central America, Australia, Visit 33				
Bible	2 Corinthians 9, 10			Life in the Word, ch. 10, lesson 4	Life in the Word, ch. 10, lesson 4
			Week 10, Lessons 166–170		
History	The Bible Smuggler, ch. 11, 12	Catch Up	Adam of the Road, ch. 21B, 22A	The Prince and the Pauper, ch. 29–31	Famous Men of the Ren and Ref, ch. 26, 27; Voices; The King's Fifth
Geography	Visits to South and Central America, Australia, Visit 34				
Bible	2 Corinthians 11			Life in the Word, ch. 11, lesson 1	Life in the Word, ch. 11, lesson 1
			Week 11, Lessons 171–175		
History	A Castle with Many Rooms, ch. 31, 32	Pippo the Fool	Adam of the Road, ch. 22B, 23	The Prince and the Pauper, ch. 32–Conclusion	Famous Men of the Ren and Ref, ch. 28, 29; Voices; The King's Fifth
Geography	Visits to South and Central America, Australia, Visit 35				
Bible	2 Corinthians 12, 13			Life in the Word, ch. 11, lesson 2	Life in the Word, ch. 11, lesson 2
			Week 12, Lessons 176–180		
History	Exams or Catch Up or Project				
Geography	Visits to South and Central America, Australia, Visit 36				
Bible	Exams or Catch Up				

 Lesson 121: Vasco Nunez de Balboa

Materials Needed

- *Around the World in a Hundred Years*
- *The Prince and the Pauper* (grades 7–9)
- *The Second Mrs. Giaconda* (grades 10–12)

Family: Ask students what they recall from last time's reading about Ponce de Leon and his explorations around Florida. Explain that today you will read about an explorer who finally made it past the Americas—well, sort of. Write "Vasco Nunez de Balboa" on the white board and read together *Around the World in a Hundred Years,* chapter 10, "Vasco Nunez de Balboa." Use the map on page 82 of that book to help students trace Balboa's explorations. Ask for an oral narration.

Grades 7–9: Read together or assign as independent reading *The Prince and the Pauper,* chapter 1, "The Birth of the Prince and the Pauper."

Grades 10–12: Assign as independent reading *The Second Mrs. Giaconda,* the first three sections ("Why, people ask," "It was hot," and "Salai was the youngest").

 Lesson 122: Various History Readings

Materials Needed

- *Marguerite Makes a Book* (grades 1–3)
- *Adam of the Road* (grades 4–6)
- *The Prince and the Pauper* (grades 7–9)
- *Famous Men of the Renaissance and Reformation* (grades 10–12)
- *The Second Mrs. Giaconda* (grades 10–12)

Grades 1–3: Read together *Marguerite Makes a Book,* part I, "In Which We Meet Marguerite, Papa Jacques, the Loathsome André, and Master Raymond."

Grades 4–6: Read together or assign as independent reading *Adam of the Road,* the first half of chapter 12, "The Ferryman's House."

Grades 7–9: Read together or assign as independent reading *The Prince and the Pauper,* chapter 2, "Tom's Early Life."

Grades 10–12: Read together or assign as independent reading *Famous Men of the Renaissance and Reformation,* chapter 8, "Sandro Botticelli," and ask for a written narration. Also assign as independent reading *The Second Mrs. Giaconda,* the next three sections ("They stayed," "Leonardo," and "The very rich").

Book of Centuries Timeline

Balboa discovers the Pacific Ocean (1513)

Sandro Botticelli, painter artist for the Medici family (1445–1510)

Book of Centuries Timeline

Lesson 123: Visit 25 to Central America & 1 Corinthians 12 and 13

Materials Needed

- *Visits to South & Central America and Australia*
- Bible
- 1 Corinthians envelope and acrostic
- *Life in the Word* (grades 7–12)

Family Geography: Complete visit 25 in *Visits to South & Central America and Australia.*

Family Bible Study: Display the 1 Corinthians envelope and acrostic paper and ask students what they recall about this epistle so far. Explain that in today's reading Paul explained how the Corinthians could use gifts from the Spirit to help each other, and especially the gift of love.

Read together 1 Corinthians 12 and 13 (or divide it into smaller portions over several days: 12:1–11, 12:12–31, 13:1–13).

Focus on 1 Corinthians 13:1–7. Discuss: What other motives might people have for sharing their knowledge or faith or possessions? How can this description of love help believers get along?

Ask students to summarize the main idea of today's passage—either what the problem was or Paul's counsel to help the Corinthians get along. Tell students to make sure their summary statement begins with the letter *A*. Record their summary statement on the paper, using the *A* as the first letter. Return the paper to the envelope for future lessons.

Grades 7–12: Help students to complete or assign as independent work *Life in the Word,* chapter 8, "Narrative Study of Acts 18," lesson 1.

Lesson 124: Ferdinand Magellan, part 1

Materials Needed

- *Around the World in a Hundred Years*
- *The Prince and the Pauper* (grades 7–9)
- *The Second Mrs. Giaconda* (grades 10–12)

Ferdinand Magellan sails around the world (1519–1522)

Family: Ask students what they recall from last time's reading about Balboa and his discovery. Explain that today you will read about an explorer who went farther than any of the others. Write "Ferdinand Magellan" on the white board and read together the first half of *Around the World in a Hundred Years,* chapter 11, "Ferdinand Magellan," about pages 95–103. Use the map on pages 6 and 7 of that book to help students trace Magellan's route. Ask for an oral narration.

Grades 7–9: Read together or assign as independent reading *The Prince and*

the Pauper, chapter 3, "Tom's Meeting with the Prince."

Grades 10–12: Assign as independent reading *The Second Mrs. Giaconda,* the next three sections ("Salai waited," "The wedding," and "From the time").

***Reminder:** Get* Castle Diary *for lesson 134 for grades 1–3 and* The King's Fifth *for lesson 134 for grades 10–12.*

 Lesson 125: Various History Readings

Materials Needed

- *Marguerite Makes a Book* (grades 1–3)
- *Adam of the Road* (grades 4–6)
- *The Prince and the Pauper* (grades 7–9)
- *Famous Men of the Renaissance and Reformation* (grades 10–12)
- *Voices of the Renaissance and Reformation* (grades 10–12)

Grades 1–3: Read together *Marguerite Makes a Book,* part II, "In Which Marguerite Meets Many People in Different Parts of Paris."

Grades 4–6: Read together or assign as independent reading *Adam of the Road,* the last half of chapter 12, "The Ferryman's House."

Grades 7–9: Read together or assign as independent reading *The Prince and the Pauper,* chapter 4, "The Prince's Troubles Begin."

Grades 10–12: Read together or assign as independent reading *Famous Men of the Renaissance and Reformation,* chapter 9, "Leonardo da Vinci," and ask for a written narration. Also assign the preface to his notebooks in *Voices of the Renaissance and Reformation,* pages 23–25.

***Tip:** Make sure older children are up to date with their* Discovering Doctrine *notebooks and their Book of Centuries entries.*

 Lesson 126: Ferdinand Magellan, part 2

Materials Needed

- *Around the World in a Hundred Years*
- *The Prince and the Pauper* (grades 7–9)
- *The Second Mrs. Giaconda* (grades 10–12)

Family: Ask students what they recall from last time's reading about Magellan's explorations so far. Explain that today you will find out what

Book of Centuries Timeline

Leonardo da Vinci, Italian painter, sculptor, architect, engineer, scientist (1452–1519)

Book of Centuries Timeline

happened on the rest of the voyage. Read together the last half of *Around the World in a Hundred Years,* chapter 11, "Ferdinand Magellan," pages 104–113. Use the map on pages 6 and 7 of that book to help students trace Magellan's route. Ask for an oral narration.

Grades 7–9: Read together or assign as independent reading *The Prince and the Pauper,* chapter 5, "Tom as a Patrician."

Grades 10–12: Assign as independent reading *The Second Mrs. Giaconda,* the next three sections ("They found," "After that day," and "Time and again").

Lesson 127: Various History Readings

Materials Needed

- *Marguerite Makes a Book* (grades 1–3)
- *Adam of the Road* (grades 4–6)
- *The Prince and the Pauper* (grades 7–9)
- *Famous Men of the Renaissance and Reformation* (grades 10–12)
- *Voices of the Renaissance and Reformation* (grades 10–12)
- *The Second Mrs. Giaconda* (grades 10–12)

Grades 1–3: Read together *Marguerite Makes a Book,* part III, "Marguerite Sets to Work."

Grades 4–6: Read together or assign as independent reading *Adam of the Road,* the first half of chapter 13, "Arrows in the King's Forest."

Grades 7–9: Read together or assign as independent reading *The Prince and the Pauper,* chapter 6, "Tom Receives Instructions."

Michelangelo Buonarroti, Italian sculptor and painter (1475–1564)

Grades 10–12: Read together or assign as independent reading *Famous Men of the Renaissance and Reformation,* chapter 10, "Michelangelo Buonarroti," and ask for a written narration. Also assign his selected poems in *Voices of the Renaissance and Reformation,* page 27.

Assign as independent reading *The Second Mrs. Giaconda,* the next two sections ("Late in the month" and "Salai missed Isabella").

Lesson 128: Visit 26 to Central America & 1 Corinthians 14

Materials Needed

- *Visits to South & Central America and Australia*
- Bible
- 1 Corinthians envelope and acrostic
- *Life in the Word* (grades 7–12)

Book of Centuries Timeline

Family Geography: Complete visit 26 in *Visits to South & Central America and Australia.*

Family Bible Study: Display the 1 Corinthians envelope and acrostic paper and ask students what they recall about this epistle so far. Explain that in today's reading Paul elaborated on how the Corinthians should be careful to care for each other when they spoke in their gatherings.

Read together 1 Corinthians 14 (or divide it into smaller portions over several days: verses 1–12, 13–25, 26–40).

Tip: Prophesying *generally involved a message given in the congregation's native language.* Tongues *involved a message given in a language that was not understood by the majority of those present; therefore, unless it was interpreted, most of the congregation couldn't benefit from it.*

Focus on 1 Corinthians 14:20. Discuss: Compare this verse with 3:1–3. How were the Corinthians being immature in their thinking? What does it mean to be an infant concerning evil? How can we take care to be that way?

Ask students to summarize the main idea of today's passage—either what the problem was or Paul's counsel to help the Corinthians get along. Tell students to make sure their summary statement begins with the letter *L*. Record their summary statement on the paper, using the *L* as the first letter. Return the paper to the envelope for future lessons.

Grades 7–12: Help students to complete or assign as independent work *Life in the Word,* chapter 8, "Narrative Study of Acts 18," lesson 2.

 Lesson 129: After Magellan

Materials Needed

- *Around the World in a Hundred Years*
- *The Stuff They Left Behind: From the Days of the Middle Ages*
- *The Prince and the Pauper* (grades 7–9)
- *The Second Mrs. Giaconda* (grades 10–12)

Family: Show students the map on pages 6 and 7 of *Around the World in a Hundred Years* and ask them to tell you what they can recall about each explorer listed there. Read together chapter 12, "After Magellan," and ask for an oral narration. Display and discuss the picture of the Moai Statues in *The Stuff They Left Behind: From the Days of the Middle Ages.*

Grades 7–9: Read together or assign as independent reading *The Prince and the Pauper,* chapter 7, "Tom's First Royal Dinner."

Grades 10–12: Assign as independent reading *The Second Mrs. Giaconda,* the next two sections ("After Beatrice" and "Salai saw even less").

Book of Centuries Timeline

Lesson 130: Various History Readings

Materials Needed

- *Marguerite Makes a Book* (grades 1–3)
- *Adam of the Road* (grades 4–6)
- *The Prince and the Pauper*, if needed (grades 7–9)
- *Famous Men of the Renaissance and Reformation* (grades 10–12)
- *The Second Mrs. Giaconda* (grades 10–12)

Grades 1–3: Read together *Marguerite Makes a Book,* part IV, "A Surprise."

Grades 4–6: Read together or assign as independent reading *Adam of the Road,* the last half of chapter 13, "Arrows in the King's Forest."

Grades 7–9: Use today to catch up on any assigned reading in *The Prince and the Pauper* if needed.

Cesare Borgia tries to take over Italy (1475–1507)

Grades 10–12: Read together or assign as independent reading *Famous Men of the Renaissance and Reformation,* chapter 11, "Cesare Borgia," and ask for a written narration. Also assign as independent reading *The Second Mrs. Giaconda,* the next three sections ("The months," "Following that evening," and "The good fortune").

***Tip:** Make sure older children are up to date with their* Discovering Doctrine *notebooks and their Book of Centuries entries.*

Lesson 131: An Explosion of Words

Materials Needed

- *A Castle with Many Rooms: The Story of the Middle Ages*
- *The Prince and the Pauper* (grades 7–9)
- *The Second Mrs. Giaconda* (grades 10–12)

Gutenberg prints the Bible using movable type (1400–1468)

Family: Explain that as Prince Henry's ships and sailors started to reach more of the world, another man in Germany invented a way for words and books to reach more of the world. Write "Gutenberg" on a small white board or sheet of paper for students to see. Read together *A Castle with Many Rooms: The Story of the Middle Ages,* chapter 27, "An Explosion of Words," and ask for an oral narration.

Grades 7–9: Read together or assign as independent reading *The Prince and the Pauper,* chapter 8, "The Question of the Seal."

Grades 10–12: Assign as independent reading the rest of *The Second Mrs. Giaconda.*

***Reminder:** Get* The Bible Smuggler *for lesson 141.*

Lesson 132: Various History Readings

Materials Needed

- *Marguerite Makes a Book,* if needed (grades 1–3)
- *Adam of the Road* (grades 4–6)
- *The Prince and the Pauper* (grades 7–9)
- *Famous Men of the Renaissance and Reformation* (grades 10–12)
- *Voices of the Renaissance and Reformation* (grades 10–12)
- *The Second Mrs. Giaconda,* if needed (grades 10–12)

Grades 1–3: Use today to catch up and finish reading *Marguerite Makes a Book* as needed.

Grades 4–6: Read together or assign as independent reading *Adam of the Road,* the first half of chapter 14, "Adam to the Rescue."

Grades 7–9: Read together or assign as independent reading *The Prince and the Pauper,* chapter 9, "The River Pageant."

Grades 10–12: Read together or assign as independent reading *Famous Men of the Renaissance and Reformation,* chapter 12, "Niccolo Machiavelli," and ask for a written narration. Also assign excerpts from "The Prince" in *Voices of the Renaissance and Reformation,* pages 29 and 30.

Use today to catch up and finish *The Second Mrs. Giaconda* if needed.

Book of Centuries Timeline

Niccolo Machiavelli writes "The Prince" (1469–1527)

Lesson 133: Visit 27 to Central America & 1 Corinthians 15

Materials Needed

- *Visits to South & Central America and Australia*
- *Material World*
- Bible
- 1 Corinthians envelope and acrostic
- *Life in the Word* (grades 7–12)

Family Geography: Complete visit 27 in *Visits to South & Central America and Australia.*

Family Bible Study: Display the 1 Corinthians envelope and acrostic paper and ask students what they recall about this epistle so far. Explain that in today's reading Paul addressed a final question the Corinthians had asked in their letter to him.

Read together 1 Corinthians 15 (or divide it into smaller portions over several days: verses 1–11, 12–34, 35–49, 50–58).

***Tip:** Most people in ancient Rome believed that after death a person just wandered in a shadowy existence in the underworld. Such belief would make suffering and enduring as a Christian futile. Paul explained*

Book of Centuries Timeline

how Christianity rests on the hope of the resurrection.

Focus on 1 Corinthians 15:51–58. Discuss: How does this passage compare with 1 Thessalonians 4:13–18? Finish this sentence: "Since Jesus is alive and those who believe in Him will live forever, ..."

Ask students to summarize the main idea of today's passage—either what the problem was or Paul's counsel to help the Corinthians. Tell students to make sure their summary statement begins with the letter *O*. Record their summary statement on the paper, using the *O* as the first letter. Return the paper to the envelope for future lessons.

Grades 7–12: Help students to complete or assign as independent work *Life in the Word,* chapter 9, "Topical Study on Weakness," lesson 1.

Lesson 134: The Conquest of Constantinople

Materials Needed

- *A Castle with Many Rooms: The Story of the Middle Ages*
- *The Stuff They Left Behind: From the Days of the Middle Ages*
- *The Prince and the Pauper* (grades 7–9)
- *The King's Fifth* (grades 10–12)

Family: Ask students what they recall from last time's reading about Gutenberg. Display the map on page 282 in *A Castle with Many Rooms,* Europe in the 14th Century, and challenge students to a little review: you will point to a place on the map and they are to tell what was happening there based on their past readings. Point in turn to Florence (Giotto's paintings spark new ideas); Switzerland (William Tell fights for freedom); England and France (100 Years War, Black Death, Joan of Arc); Portugal (Prince Henry's ships explore the coast of Africa). Have students find Constantinople and explain that today's reading will tell them what was happening over there. Read together *A Castle with Many Rooms: The Story of the Middle Ages,* chapter 28, "The Conquest of Constantinople," and ask for an oral narration. Display and discuss the picture of Hagia Sophia in *The Stuff They Left Behind: From the Days of the Middle Ages.*

Constantinople conquered by Ottomans, becomes Istanbul; end of the Eastern Roman Empire (1453)

Grades 7–9: Read together or assign as independent reading *The Prince and the Pauper,* chapter 10, "The Prince in the Toils."

Grades 10–12: Assign as independent reading *The King's Fifth,* Diary Entry 1 and chapter 1.

Lesson 135: Various History Readings

Materials Needed

- *Castle Diary* (grades 1–3)

- *Adam of the Road* (grades 4–6)
- *The Prince and the Pauper* (grades 7–9)
- *Famous Men of the Renaissance and Reformation* (grades 10–12)
- *The King's Fifth* (grades 10–12)

Grades 1–3: Read together *Castle Diary,* from the beginning of Tobias' journal through January 13.

Grades 4–6: Read together or assign as independent reading *Adam of the Road,* the last half of chapter 14, "Adam to the Rescue."

Grades 7–9: Read together or assign as independent reading *The Prince and the Pauper,* chapter 11, "At Guildhall."

Grades 10–12: Read together or assign as independent reading *Famous Men of the Renaissance and Reformation,* chapter 13, "Leo X (Giovanni de' Medici)," and ask for a written narration. Also assign as independent reading *The King's Fifth,* chapters 2 and 3.

***Tip:** Make sure older children are up to date with their* Discovering Doctrine *notebooks and their Book of Centuries entries.*

Book of Centuries Timeline

Giovanni de'Medici becomes Leo X (1475–1521)

Lesson 136: Rebirth

Materials Needed
- *A Castle with Many Rooms: The Story of the Middle Ages*
- *The Prince and the Pauper* (grades 7–9)
- *The King's Fifth* (grades 10–12)

Family: Ask students what they recall from last time's reading about the fall of Constantinople. Display the map on page 282 in *A Castle with Many Rooms* and have them find Florence. Explain that today they will hear about more of the changes that were happening there. Read together *A Castle with Many Rooms: The Story of the Middle Ages,* chapter 29, "Rebirth." Write the following names on a small white board or sheet of paper as you come to them in the chapter: "Giotto," "Medici," "Michelangelo," "Leonardo da Vinci," "Petrarch." Ask for an oral narration.

Grades 7–9: Read together or assign as independent reading *The Prince and the Pauper,* the first half of chapter 12, "The Prince and His Deliverer."

Grades 10–12: Assign as independent reading *The King's Fifth,* chapters 4 and 5.

Lesson 137: Various History Readings

Materials Needed
- *Castle Diary* (grades 1–3)

Book of Centuries Timeline

- *Adam of the Road* (grades 4–6)
- *The Prince and the Pauper* (grades 7–9)
- *Famous Men of the Renaissance and Reformation* (grades 10–12)
- *Voices of the Renaissance and Reformation* (grades 10–12)
- *The King's Fifth* (grades 10–12)

Grades 1–3: Read together *Castle Diary,* from January 14 through January 23.

Grades 4–6: Read together or assign as independent reading *Adam of the Road,* the first half of chapter 15, "St. Gile's Fair."

Grades 7–9: Read together or assign as independent reading *The Prince and the Pauper,* the last half of chapter 12, "The Prince and His Deliverer."

Erasmus tries to reform the Roman church from within (1466–1536)

Grades 10–12: Read together or assign as independent reading *Famous Men of the Renaissance and Reformation,* chapter 14, "Erasmus," and ask for a written narration. Also assign the preface to "In Praise of Folly" in *Voices of the Renaissance and Reformation,* pages 31 and 32.

Assign as independent reading *The King's Fifth,* Diary Entry 2 and chapter 6.

Lesson 138: Visit 28 to Central America & 1 Corinthians 16

Materials Needed

- *Visits to South & Central America and Australia*
- Bible
- 1 Corinthians envelope and acrostic
- *Life in the Word* (grades 7–12)

Family Geography: Complete visit 28 in *Visits to South & Central America and Australia.*

Family Bible Study: Display the 1 Corinthians envelope and acrostic paper and ask students what they recall about this epistle. Explain that in today's reading Paul wrapped things up with some final instructions and comments.

Read together 1 Corinthians 16 (or divide it into smaller portions over several days: verses 1–11, 12–24).

Focus on 1 Corinthians 16:13 and 14. Discuss: Take each phrase in these verses and explain how obeying it would contribute to getting along in God's family.

Ask students to summarize the main idea of today's passage—either what the problem was or Paul's counsel to help the Corinthians get along. Tell students to make sure their summary statement begins with the letter *N*. Record their summary statement on the paper, using the *N* as the first letter.

Book of Centuries Timeline

Ask students if there is anything else they would like to add to their summary of 1 Corinthians. The final *G* line is still available. If they don't have another statement, write "Getting Along" again for the bottom line. Return the paper to the envelope.

Grades 7–12: Help students to complete or assign as independent work *Life in the Word,* chapter 9, "Topical Study on Weakness," lesson 2.

 Lesson 139: Reformation

Materials Needed

- *A Castle with Many Rooms: The Story of the Middle Ages*
- *The Prince and the Pauper* (grades 7–9)
- *The King's Fifth* (grades 10–12)

Family: Ask students what they recall from last time's reading about the Renaissance. Explain that the winds of ideas from the Renaissance caused people to think deeply about things around them. One such person, a monk in Germany, began an argument that eventually spread over the world. Read together *A Castle with Many Rooms: The Story of the Middle Ages,* chapter 30, "Reformation," and ask for an oral narration.

Martin Luther of Germany posts his 95 Theses and ignites the Protestant Reformation (1517)

Grades 7–9: Read together or assign as independent reading *The Prince and the Pauper,* the first half of chapter 13, "The Disappearance of the Prince."

Grades 10–12: Assign as independent reading *The King's Fifth,* chapters 7 and 8.

 Lesson 140: Various History Readings

Materials Needed

- *Castle Diary* (grades 1–3)
- *Adam of the Road* (grades 4–6)
- *The Prince and the Pauper* (grades 7–9)
- *Famous Men of the Renaissance and Reformation* (grades 10–12)
- *Voices of the Renaissance and Reformation* (grades 10–12)
- *The King's Fifth* (grades 10–12)

Grades 1–3: Read together *Castle Diary,* from January 24 through January 27.

Grades 4–6: Read together or assign as independent reading *Adam of the Road,* the last half of chapter 15, "St. Gile's Fair."

Grades 7–9: Read together or assign as independent reading *The Prince and the Pauper,* the last half of chapter 13, "The Disappearance of the Prince."

Grades 10–12: Read together or assign as independent reading *Famous*

Book of Centuries Timeline

John Wyclif translates the Latin Vulgate into English (1330–1384)

Men of the Renaissance and Reformation, chapter 15, "John Wyclif," and ask for a written narration. Also assign the charges against him and his reply in *Voices of the Renaissance and Reformation,* pages 33–35.

Assign as independent reading *The King's Fifth,* chapter 9 and Diary Entry 3.

***Tip:** Make sure older children are up to date with their* Discovering Doctrine *notebooks and their Book of Centuries entries.*

Lesson 141: Tyndale, part 1

Materials Needed

- *The Bible Smuggler*
- *The Prince and the Pauper* (grades 7–9)
- *The King's Fifth* (grades 10–12)

Family: Ask students what they recall from last time's reading about Martin Luther. Explain that men in many countries agreed with Luther and were not afraid to say so, which often put them in danger. One such man was named William Tyndale. His great desire was to translate the Bible into English, just as Luther had translated it into German, so the common people could read it in a language they understood. But Church authorities did not agree. Read together *The Bible Smuggler,* chapter 1, "Death Before the Feast."

Grades 7–9: Read together or assign as independent reading *The Prince and the Pauper,* the first half of chapter 14, "Le Roi Est Mort! Vive Le Roi."

Grades 10–12: Assign as independent reading *The King's Fifth,* chapter 10.

Lesson 142: Various History Readings

Materials Needed

- *Castle Diary* (grades 1–3)
- *Adam of the Road* (grades 4–6)
- *The Prince and the Pauper* (grades 7–9)
- *Famous Men of the Renaissance and Reformation* (grades 10–12)
- *Voices of the Renaissance and Reformation* (grades 10–12)
- *The King's Fifth* (grades 10–12)

Grades 1–3: Read together *Castle Diary,* from February 5 through February 22.

Grades 4–6: Read together or assign as independent reading *Adam of the Road,* chapter 16, "The Fall of Adam."

Grades 7–9: Read together or assign as independent reading *The Prince and*

the Pauper, the last half of chapter 14, "Le Roi Est Mort! Vive Le Roi."

Grades 10–12: Read together or assign as independent reading *Famous Men of the Renaissance and Reformation,* chapter 16, "Jan Hus," and ask for a written narration. Also assign his final declaration in *Voices of the Renaissance and Reformation,* page 37.

Assign as independent reading *The King's Fifth,* chapter 11.

Book of Centuries Timeline

Jan Hus of Bohemia condemns Church abuse; burned at the stake (1374–1415)

Lesson 143: Visit 29 to the Caribbean & 2 Corinthians 1 and 2

Materials Needed

- *Visits to South & Central America and Australia*
- Bible
- Map of Paul's Journeys
- Envelope with labeled paper
- *Life in the Word* (grades 7–12)

Family Geography: Complete visit 29 in *Visits to South & Central America and Australia.*

Family Bible Study: Before the lesson begins, write "Courage" on a paper and put it in an envelope. Ask students what they recall about the epistle called 1 Corinthians. Explain that many of the Corinthian believers responded to Paul's letter and repented. Others, however, did not, choosing instead to believe Paul's enemies, who spread lies about him and the gospel. So Paul sent another letter from Macedonia. (Help students locate it on a map of Paul's journeys.) In this letter he commended those who had repented, then continued to defend his calling as an apostle of the Lord Jesus and the truth of the gospel.

Paul writes 2 Corinthians from Macedonia (c. 55–56)

Help students address the new envelope to reflect 2 Corinthians, then invite them to read the labeled paper you put inside it. Explain that much of Paul's message in this letter involves courage. Discuss: What is courage? What kinds of hard things might require courage?

Encourage students to listen for circumstances or actions that would involve courage. Read together 2 Corinthians 1 and 2 (or divide it into smaller portions over several days: 1:1–11, 1:12–24, 2:1–11, 2:12–17).

Focus on 2 Corinthians 2:5–8. Discuss: Why does it take courage to forgive someone who has caused you pain? How can you know if that person is truly repentant?

Ask students to summarize the main ideas of today's passage. Discuss how those ideas might involve courage. Record students' findings on the Courage paper and return it to the envelope for future lessons.

Grades 7–12: Help students to complete or assign as independent work *Life in the Word,* chapter 9, "Topical Study on Weakness," lesson 3.

Book of Centuries Timeline

Lesson 144: Tyndale, part 2

Materials Needed

- *The Bible Smuggler*
- *The Prince and the Pauper* (grades 7–9)
- *The King's Fifth* (grades 10–12)

Family: Ask students where you left off in the story of Tyndale last time. Read together *The Bible Smuggler,* chapter 2, "Secret Trial."

Grades 7–9: Read together or assign as independent reading *The Prince and the Pauper*, the first half of chapter 15, "Tom as King."

Grades 10–12: Assign as independent reading *The King's Fifth,* chapter 12 and Diary Entry 4.

Lesson 145: Various History Readings

Materials Needed

- *Castle Diary* (grades 1–3)
- *Adam of the Road* (grades 4–6)
- *The Prince and the Pauper* (grades 7–9)
- *Famous Men of the Renaissance and Reformation* (grades 10–12)

Grades 1–3: Read together *Castle Diary,* from March 3 through March 20.

Grades 4–6: Read together or assign as independent reading *Adam of the Road,* the first half of chapter 17, "Adam Meets Some Minstrels."

Grades 7–9: Read together or assign as independent reading *The Prince and the Pauper,* the last half of chapter 15, "Tom as King."

Grades 10–12: Read together or assign as independent reading *Famous Men of the Renaissance and Reformation,* chapter 17, "Martin Luther," and ask for a written narration.

Tip: *Make sure older children are up to date with their* Discovering Doctrine *notebooks and their Book of Centuries entries.*

Lesson 146: Tyndale, part 3

Materials Needed

- *The Bible Smuggler*
- *The Prince and the Pauper* (grades 7–9)
- *Voices of the Renaissance and Reformation* (grades 10–12)

Family: Ask students where you left off in the story of Tyndale last time. Read together *The Bible Smuggler,* chapter 3, "No Room for Heretics."

Grades 7–9: Read together or assign as independent reading *The Prince and the Pauper,* chapter 16, "The State Dinner."

Grades 10–12: Read together or assign as independent reading Luther's preface in *Voices of the Renaissance and Reformation,* pages 39–47. Also look over his 95 Theses on pages 49–55. (Feel free to assign any other of his writings that you desire, as well.)

Book of Centuries Timeline

Lesson 147: Various History Readings

Materials Needed

- *Castle Diary* (grades 1–3)
- *Adam of the Road* (grades 4–6)
- *The Prince and the Pauper* (grades 7–9)
- *Famous Men of the Renaissance and Reformation* (grades 10–12)
- *The King's Fifth* (grades 10–12)

Grades 1–3: Read together *Castle Diary,* from April 11 through April 26

Grades 4–6: Read together or assign as independent reading *Adam of the Road,* the last half of chapter 17, "Adam Meets Some Minstrels."

Grades 7–9: Read together or assign as independent reading *The Prince and the Pauper,* chapter 17, "Foo-Foo the First."

Grades 10–12: Read together or assign as independent reading *Famous Men of the Renaissance and Reformation,* chapter 18, "Charles V," and ask for a written narration.

Assign as independent reading *The King's Fifth,* chapter 13.

Charles V, King of Spain, crowned Holy Roman Emperor (1500–1558)

Lesson 148: Visit 30 to the Caribbean & 2 Corinthians 3 and 4

Materials Needed

- *Visits to South & Central America and Australia*
- *Material World*
- Bible
- 2 Corinthians envelope with Courage paper
- *Life in the Word* (grades 7–12)

Family Geography: Complete visit 30 in *Visits to South & Central America and Australia.*

Family Bible Study: Display the 2 Corinthians envelope and Courage paper

Book of Centuries Timeline

and ask students what they recall about this epistle so far. Explain that in today's reading Paul addressed some of the false accusations that had been leveled against him. Some people were casting doubt at him because he didn't have any letters of recommendation.

Read together 2 Corinthians 3 and 4 (or divide it into smaller portions over several days: 3:1–6, 3:7–18, 4:1–6, 4:7–18). Encourage students to listen for circumstances or actions that would involve courage.

Focus on 2 Corinthians 4:16–18. Discuss: In the midst of the accusations, why did Paul not lose hope? How can verse 18 give us courage?

Ask students to summarize the main ideas of today's passage. Discuss how those ideas might involve courage. Record students' findings on the Courage paper and return it to the envelope for future lessons.

Grades 7–12: Help students to complete or assign as independent work *Life in the Word,* chapter 10, "Inductive Study of 2 Corinthians 4," lesson 1.

 Lesson 149: Tyndale, part 4

Materials Needed

- *The Bible Smuggler*
- *The Prince and the Pauper* (grades 7–9)
- *The King's Fifth* (grades 10–12)

Family: Ask students where you left off in the story of Tyndale last time. Read together *The Bible Smuggler,* chapter 4, "Unwilling Witness."

Grades 7–9: Read together or assign as independent reading *The Prince and the Pauper,* chapter 18, "The Prince with the Tramps."

Grades 10–12: Assign as independent reading *The King's Fifth,* chapters 14 and 15.

 Lesson 150: Various History Readings

Materials Needed

- *Castle Diary* (grades 1–3)
- *Adam of the Road* (grades 4–6)
- *The Prince and the Pauper,* if needed (grades 7–9)
- *Famous Men of the Renaissance and Reformation* (grades 10–12)
- *The King's Fifth* (grades 10–12)

Grades 1–3: Read together *Castle Diary,* from May 3 through June 15.

Grades 4–6: Read together or assign as independent reading *Adam of the Road,* the first half of chapter 18, "Hue and Cry."

Grades 7–9: Use today to catch up on any assigned reading in *The Prince and the Pauper* if needed.

Grades 10–12: Read together or assign as independent reading *Famous Men of the Renaissance and Reformation,* chapter 19, "Albrecht Dürer," and ask for a written narration.

Assign as independent reading *The King's Fifth,* chapters 16 and 17.

Tip: Make sure older children are up to date with their Discovering Doctrine *notebooks and their Book of Centuries entries.*

Book of Centuries Timeline

Albrecht Dürer, German artist and engraver (1471–1528)

 Lesson 151: Tyndale, part 5

Materials Needed

- *The Bible Smuggler*
- *The Prince and the Pauper* (grades 7–9)
- *The King's Fifth* (grades 10–12)

Family: Ask students where you left off in the story of Tyndale last time. Read together *The Bible Smuggler,* chapter 5, "Invitation to Leave."

Grades 7–9: Read together or assign as independent reading *The Prince and the Pauper,* chapter 19, "The Prince with the Peasants."

Grades 10–12: Assign as independent reading *The King's Fifth,* chapter 18.

 Lesson 152: Various History Readings

Materials Needed

- *Castle Diary* (grades 1–3)
- *Adam of the Road* (grades 4–6)
- *The Prince and the Pauper* (grades 7–9)
- *Famous Men of the Renaissance and Reformation* (grades 10–12)
- *Voices of the Renaissance and Reformation* (grades 10–12)

Grades 1–3: Read together *Castle Diary,* from June 20 through August 7.

Grades 4–6: Read together or assign as independent reading *Adam of the Road,* the last half of chapter 18, "Hue and Cry."

Grades 7–9: Read together or assign as independent reading *The Prince and the Pauper,* chapter 20, "The Prince and the Hermit."

Grades 10–12: Read together or assign as independent reading *Famous Men of the Renaissance and Reformation,* chapter 20, "Ulrich Zwingli," and ask for a written narration. Also look over his 67 Articles in *Voices of the Renaissance and Reformation,* pages 117–122.

Ulrich Zwingli carries the Reformation to Switzerland (1484–1531)

Book of Centuries Timeline

Lesson 153: Visit 31 to the Caribbean & 2 Corinthians 5 and 6

Materials Needed

- *Visits to South & Central America and Australia*
- *Hungry Planet: What the World Eats*
- Bible
- 2 Corinthians envelope with Courage paper
- *Life in the Word* (grades 7–12)

Family Geography: Complete visit 31 in *Visits to South & Central America and Australia.*

Family Bible Study: Display the 2 Corinthians envelope and Courage paper and ask students what they recall about this epistle so far. Explain that in today's reading Paul explained why outward appearance should make no difference in ministry and urged the Corinthians to look at heart issues, instead, as they chose who to follow.

Read together 2 Corinthians 5 and 6 (or divide it into smaller portions over several days: 5:1–10, 5:11–21, 6:1–13, 6:14–18). Encourage students to listen for circumstances or actions that would involve courage.

Focus on 2 Corinthians 6:14 and 15. Discuss: What is a yoke? What would "unequally yoked" mean? What should our focus be when selecting close leaders and friends? Does it take courage to focus on heart issues rather than appearance in choosing our friends? Why?

Ask students to summarize the main ideas of today's passage. Discuss how those ideas might involve courage. Record students' findings on the Courage paper and return it to the envelope for future lessons.

Grades 7–12: Help students to complete or assign as independent work *Life in the Word,* chapter 10, "Inductive Study of 2 Corinthians 4," lesson 2.

Lesson 154: Tyndale, part 6

Materials Needed

- *The Bible Smuggler*
- *The Prince and the Pauper* (grades 7–9)
- *The King's Fifth* (grades 10–12)

Family: Ask students where you left off in the story of Tyndale last time. Read together *The Bible Smuggler,* chapter 6, "Inspired Flight."

Grades 7–9: Read together or assign as independent reading *The Prince and the Pauper,* chapter 21, "Hendon to the Rescue."

Grades 10–12: Assign as independent reading *The King's Fifth,* Diary Entry 5.

Book of Centuries Timeline

Lesson 155: Various History Readings

Materials Needed

- *Castle Diary* (grades 1–3)
- *Adam of the Road* (grades 4–6)
- *The Prince and the Pauper*, if needed (grades 7–9)
- *Famous Men of the Renaissance and Reformation* (grades 10–12)
- *The King's Fifth* (grades 10–12)

Grades 1–3: Read together *Castle Diary,* from August 8 through August 16.

Tip: *In the entry for August 8, the other pages make fun of Toby for sitting immodestly. The wording is not at all inappropriate, but you can easily skip that section of the entry if desired.*

Grades 4–6: Read together or assign as independent reading *Adam of the Road,* the first half of chapter 19, "News of Roger."

Grades 7–9: Use today to catch up on any assigned reading in *The Prince and the Pauper* if needed.

Grades 10–12: Read together or assign as independent reading *Famous Men of the Renaissance and Reformation,* chapter 21, "Thomas Muntzer," and ask for a written narration.

Assign as independent reading *The King's Fifth,* chapters 19 and 20.

Tip: *Make sure older children are up to date with their* Discovering Doctrine *notebooks and their Book of Centuries entries.*

Lesson 156: Tyndale, part 7

Materials Needed

- *The Bible Smuggler*
- *The Prince and the Pauper* (grades 7–9)
- *The King's Fifth* (grades 10–12)

Family: Ask students where you left off in the story of Tyndale last time. Read together *The Bible Smuggler,* chapter 7, "Two Strangers."

Grades 7–9: Read together or assign as independent reading *The Prince and the Pauper,* chapter 22, "A Victim of Treachery."

Grades 10–12: Assign as independent reading *The King's Fifth,* Diary Entry 6 and chapter 21.

Book of Centuries Timeline

Lesson 157: Various History Readings

Materials Needed

- *Castle Diary* (grades 1–3)
- *Adam of the Road* (grades 4–6)
- *The Prince and the Pauper* (grades 7–9)
- *Famous Men of the Renaissance and Reformation* (grades 10–12)
- *Voices of the Renaissance and Reformation* (grades 10–12)
- *The King's Fifth*, if needed (grades 10–12)

Grades 1–3: Read together *Castle Diary,* from August 24 through September 3.

Grades 4–6: Read together or assign as independent reading *Adam of the Road,* the last half of chapter 19, "News of Roger."

Grades 7–9: Read together or assign as independent reading *The Prince and the Pauper,* chapter 23, "The Prince a Prisoner."

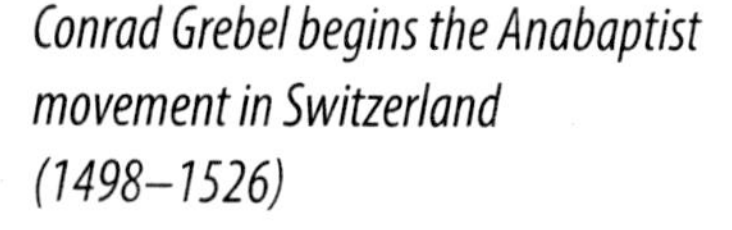

Conrad Grebel begins the Anabaptist movement in Switzerland (1498–1526)

Michael Sattler, Anabaptist martyr in Switzerland (1490?–1527)

Grades 10–12: Read together or assign as independent reading *Famous Men of the Renaissance and Reformation,* chapter 22, "Conrad Grebel and Michael Sattler," and ask for a written narration. Also assign Grebel's Letters to Muntzer in *Voices of the Renaissance and Reformation,* pages 123–131, and The Trial of Michael Sattler, pages 137–140.

Use today to catch up on any assigned reading in *The King's Fifth* if needed.

Lesson 158: Visit 32 to the Caribbean & 2 Corinthians 7 and 8

Materials Needed

- *Visits to South & Central America and Australia*
- Bible
- 2 Corinthians envelope with Courage paper
- *Life in the Word* (grades 7–12)

Family Geography: Complete visit 32 in *Visits to South & Central America and Australia.*

Family Bible Study: Display the 2 Corinthians envelope and Courage paper and ask students what they recall about this epistle so far. Explain that in today's reading Paul reaffirmed his confidence in the believers at Corinth and encouraged them to demonstrate their repentance by giving to other believers in need.

Read together 2 Corinthians 7 and 8 (or divide it into smaller portions over several days: 7:1–9, 7:10–16, 8:1–15, 8:16–24). Encourage students to listen for circumstances or actions that would involve courage.

Focus on 2 Corinthians 7:9 and 10. Discuss: What do we usually feel when someone points out how we were wrong? What is the difference between godly grief and worldly grief? How will godly grief show? Do you think it requires courage to repent when someone points out how you were wrong? Why?

Ask students to summarize the main ideas of today's passage. Discuss how those ideas might involve courage. Record students' findings on the Courage paper and return it to the envelope for future lessons.

Grades 7–12: Help students to complete or assign as independent work *Life in the Word,* chapter 10, "Inductive Study of 2 Corinthians 4," lesson 3.

Book of Centuries Timeline

Lesson 159: Tyndale, part 8

Materials Needed

- *The Bible Smuggler*
- *The Stuff They Left Behind: From the Days of the Middle Ages*
- *The Prince and the Pauper* (grades 7–9)
- *The King's Fifth* (grades 10–12)

Family: Explain that while William Tyndale was living in Europe, a group of people were living in very different lodgings in North America. Display and discuss the picture of the Cliff Palace at Mesa Verde in *The Stuff They Left Behind: From the Days of the Middle Ages.*

Ask students where you left off in the story of Tyndale last time. Read together *The Bible Smuggler,* chapter 8, "Unseen Visitors."

Grades 7–9: Read together or assign as independent reading *The Prince and the Pauper,* chapter 24, "The Escape."

Grades 10–12: Assign as independent reading *The King's Fifth,* chapters 22 and 23.

Lesson 160: Various History Readings

Materials Needed

- *Castle Diary* (grades 1–3)
- *Adam of the Road* (grades 4–6)
- *The Prince and the Pauper* (grades 7–9)
- *Famous Men of the Renaissance and Reformation* (grades 10–12)
- *The King's Fifth* (grades 10–12)

Grades 1–3: Read together *Castle Diary,* from September 4 through November 9.

Grades 4–6: Read together or assign as independent reading *Adam of the Road,* the first half of chapter 20, "What Have You Done with Him?"

Grades 7–9: Read together or assign as independent reading *The Prince and*

the Pauper, chapter 25, "Hendon Hall."

Grades 10–12: Read together or assign as independent reading *Famous Men of the Renaissance and Reformation,* chapter 23, "Melchior Hoffman, Jan Matthys, and Menno Simons," and ask for a written narration.
Assign as independent reading *The King's Fifth,* chapters 24 and 25.

Book of Centuries Timeline

Menno Simons published Anabaptist "Book of Fundamentals"; founds Mennonites (1496–1561)

Tip: Make sure older children are up to date with their Discovering Doctrine *notebooks and their Book of Centuries entries.*

 Lesson 161: Tyndale, part 9

Materials Needed
- *The Bible Smuggler*
- *The Prince and the Pauper* (grades 7–9)
- *The King's Fifth* (grades 10–12)

Family: Ask students where you left off in the story of Tyndale last time. Read together *The Bible Smuggler,* chapter 9, "The Forbidden Book."

Grades 7–9: Read together or assign as independent reading *The Prince and the Pauper,* chapter 26, "Disowned."

Grades 10–12: Assign as independent reading *The King's Fifth,* Diary Entry 7.

 Lesson 162: Various History Readings

Materials Needed
- *Castle Diary* (grades 1–3)
- *Adam of the Road* (grades 4–6)
- *The Prince and the Pauper* (grades 7–9)
- *Famous Men of the Renaissance and Reformation* (grades 10–12)
- *Voices of the Renaissance and Reformation* (grades 10–12)

Grades 1–3: Read together *Castle Diary,* from November 22 through December 28.

Grades 4–6: Read together or assign as independent reading *Adam of the Road,* the last half of chapter 20, "What Have You Done with Him?"

Grades 7–9: Read together or assign as independent reading *The Prince and the Pauper,* chapter 27, "In Prison."

Henry VIII breaks from Roman church to be declared head of Church of England (1491–1547)

Grades 10–12: Read together or assign as independent reading *Famous Men of the Renaissance and Reformation,* chapter 24, "Henry VIII," and ask for a written narration.
Assign as independent reading *The King's Fifth,* chapters 26 and 27.

Book of Centuries
Timeline

Reminder: *Get* Pippo the Fool *for lesson 172 for grades 1–3.*

Lesson 163: Visit 33 to the Caribbean & 2 Corinthians 9 and 10

Materials Needed

- *Visits to South & Central America and Australia*
- *Material World*
- Bible
- 2 Corinthians envelope with Courage paper
- *Life in the Word* (grades 7–12)

Family Geography: Complete visit 33 in *Visits to South & Central America and Australia.*

Family Bible Study: Display the 2 Corinthians envelope and Courage paper and ask students what they recall about this epistle so far. Explain that in today's reading Paul challenged the Corinthians to give generously then defended himself against the accusation that he put on a show of meekness when he was with them but wrote scathingly bold letters.

Read together 2 Corinthians 9 and 10 (or divide it into smaller portions over several days: 9:1–5, 9:6–15, 10:1–6, 10:7–18). Encourage students to listen for circumstances or actions that would involve courage.

Focus on 2 Corinthians 9:6–8. Discuss: Does it take courage to give generously? Why? These sentences applaud some attitudes behind the giving? Why would those attitudes be so important?

Ask students to summarize the main ideas of today's passage. Discuss how those ideas might involve courage. Record students' findings on the Courage paper and return it to the envelope for future lessons.

Grades 7–12: Help students to complete or assign as independent work *Life in the Word,* chapter 10, "Inductive Study of 2 Corinthians 4," lesson 4.

Lesson 164: Tyndale, part 10

Materials Needed

- *The Bible Smuggler*
- *The Prince and the Pauper* (grades 7–9)
- *The King's Fifth* (grades 10–12)

Family: Ask students where you left off in the story of Tyndale last time. Read together *The Bible Smuggler,* chapter 10, "Daring Journey."

Grades 7–9: Read together or assign as independent reading *The Prince and the Pauper,* chapter 28, "The Sacrifice."

Book of Centuries Timeline

Grades 10–12: Assign as independent reading *The King's Fifth,* chapters 28 and 29.

 Lesson 165: Various History Readings

Materials Needed

- *Castle Diary* (grades 1–3)
- *Adam of the Road* (grades 4–6)
- *The Prince and the Pauper*, if needed (grades 7–9)
- *Famous Men of the Renaissance and Reformation* (grades 10–12)
- *Voices of the Renaissance and Reformation* (grades 10–12)
- *The King's Fifth* (grades 10–12)

Grades 1–3: Use today to catch up on *Castle Diary* or to read a portion of "Toby's World" at the end if desired. (You will have another opportunity to do this in lesson 167.)

Grades 4–6: Read together or assign as independent reading *Adam of the Road,* the first half of chapter 21, "Adam's Song."

Grades 7–9: Use today to catch up on any assigned reading in *The Prince and the Pauper* if needed.

Grades 10–12: Read together or assign as independent reading *Famous Men of the Renaissance and Reformation,* chapter 25, "Thomas More," and ask for a written narration. Also assign his letter to his daughter in *Voices of the Renaissance and Reformation,* page 159.

Thomas More, Henry VIII's Lord Chancellor (1477–1535)

Assign as independent reading *The King's Fifth,* Diary Entry 8.

Tip: Make sure older children are up to date with their Discovering Doctrine *notebooks and their Book of Centuries entries.*

 Lesson 166: Tyndale, part 11

Materials Needed

- *The Bible Smuggler*
- *The Prince and the Pauper* (grades 7–9)
- *The King's Fifth* (grades 10–12)

Family: Ask students where you left off in the story of Tyndale last time. Read together *The Bible Smuggler,* chapter 11, "The Hidden Word."

William Tyndale publishes first complete Bible in English (1495–1536)

Grades 7–9: Read together or assign as independent reading *The Prince and the Pauper,* chapter 29, "To London."

Grades 10–12: Assign as independent reading *The King's Fifth,* chapters 30 and 31.

Book of Centuries
Timeline

Lesson 167: Various History Readings

Materials Needed

- *Castle Diary* (grades 1–3)
- *Adam of the Road* (grades 4–6)
- *The Prince and the Pauper* (grades 7–9)
- *Famous Men of the Renaissance and Reformation* (grades 10–12)

Grades 1–3: Use today to catch up on *Castle Diary* or to read a portion of "Toby's World" at the end if desired.

Grades 4–6: Read together or assign as independent reading *Adam of the Road,* the last half of chapter 21, "Adam's Song."

Grades 7–9: Read together or assign as independent reading *The Prince and the Pauper,* chapter 30, "Tom's Progress."

Grades 10–12: Read together or assign as independent reading *Famous Men of the Renaissance and Reformation,* chapter 26, "William Tyndale," and ask for a written narration.

Lesson 168: Visit 34 to the Caribbean & 2 Corinthians 11

Materials Needed

- *Visits to South & Central America and Australia*
- Bible
- 2 Corinthians envelope with Courage paper
- *Life in the Word* (grades 7–12)

Family Geography: Complete visit 34 in *Visits to South & Central America and Australia.*

Family Bible Study: Display the 2 Corinthians envelope and Courage paper and ask students what they recall about this epistle so far. Explain that in today's reading Paul reluctantly listed his qualifications as an apostle. The unrepentant Corinthians were following false leaders because they thought them more qualified. If Paul were going to bring them back to the true gospel that he preached, he would have to convince them that he was worthy of being their leader, though he felt foolish doing so.

Read together 2 Corinthians 11 (or divide it into smaller portions over several days: verses 1–15, 16–33). Encourage students to listen for circumstances or actions that would involve courage.

Focus on 2 Corinthians 11. Discuss: Which of Paul's experiences as a follower of Jesus do you think required the most courage? What can we learn from his sufferings and endurance?

Ask students to summarize the main ideas of today's passage. Discuss how those ideas might involve courage. Record students' findings on the

Book of Centuries Timeline

Courage paper and return it to the envelope for future lessons.

Grades 7–12: Help students to complete or assign as independent work *Life in the Word,* chapter 11, "Character Study on Titus," lesson 1.

 Lesson 169: Tyndale, part 12

Materials Needed

- *The Bible Smuggler*
- *The Prince and the Pauper* (grades 7–9)
- *Voices of the Renaissance and Reformation* (grades 10–12)

Family: Ask students where you left off in the story of Tyndale last time. Read together *The Bible Smuggler,* chapter 12, "Glorious Exile."

Grades 7–9: Read together or assign as independent reading *The Prince and the Pauper,* chapter 31, "The Recognition Procession."

Grades 10–12: Assign John Tyndale's Preface to His Commentary on the Psalms in *Voices of the Renaissance and Reformation,* pages 145–152.

Reminder: *If you want to do a hands-on project for lessons 176–180, gather any supplies you might need.*

 Lesson 170: Various History Readings

Materials Needed

- *Castle Diary*, if needed (grades 1–3)
- *Adam of the Road* (grades 4–6)
- *The Prince and the Pauper*, if needed (grades 7–9)
- *Famous Men of the Renaissance and Reformation* (grades 10–12)
- *Voices of the Renaissance and Reformation* (grades 10–12)

Grades 1–3: Use today to catch up and finish reading *Castle Diary* as needed.

Grades 4–6: Read together or assign as independent reading *Adam of the Road,* the first half of chapter 22, "Adam Helps a Plowman."

Grades 7–9: Use today to catch up on any assigned reading in *The Prince and the Pauper* if needed.

Thomas Cromwell, Henry VIII's principal secretary, dissolves monasteries in England (1485–1540)

Thomas Cranmer, Archbishop of Canterbury, encourages Henry VIII to approve English Bible (1489–1556)

Grades 10–12: Read together or assign as independent reading *Famous Men of the Renaissance and Reformation,* chapter 27, "Thomas Cromwell and Thomas Cranmer," and ask for a written narration. Also assign the two Acts of Henry VIII and Thomas Cromwell in *Voices of the Renaissance and Reformation,* pages 153–158.

Tip: Make sure older children are up to date with their Discovering Doctrine *notebooks and their Book of Centuries entries.*

Book of Centuries Timeline

Lesson 171: Revolution

Materials Needed

- *A Castle with Many Rooms: The Story of the Middle Ages*
- *The Prince and the Pauper* (grades 7–9)
- *The King's Fifth* (grades 10–12)

Family: Write on a small white board or sheet of paper "Renaissance," "Reformation," and "Exploration." Ask students what they recall about those three changes that were sweeping across the world. Guide them to see which areas of life were affected by each change; e.g., art, architecture, religion, geography, trade relations. Look together at the map of Europe in the 15th Century (page 283 in *A Castle with Many Rooms*) and compare it to the map of Europe in the Time of Odoacer (page 274). Let students notice how much things changed during the Middle Ages. Add the word "Revolution" to the list and explain that in today's reading they will hear about one more sweeping change; this time in the world of science. Write "scientific" in front of "revolution," so it reads "Scientific Revolution." Read together *A Castle with Many Rooms: The Story of the Middle Ages,* chapter 31, "Revolution," and ask for an oral narration.

Copernicus writes The Revolutions of the Celestial Spheres, proposing that the earth orbits the sun (1532)

Grades 7–9: Read together or assign as independent reading *The Prince and the Pauper,* chapter 32, "Coronation Day."

Grades 10–12: Assign as independent reading *The King's Fifth,* final Diary Entry.

Lesson 172: Various History Readings

Materials Needed

- *Pippo the Fool* (grades 1–3)
- *Adam of the Road* (grades 4–6)
- *The Prince and the Pauper* (grades 7–9)
- *Famous Men of the Renaissance and Reformation* (grades 10–12)

Grades 1–3: Read together *Pippo the Fool.*

Grades 4–6: Read together or assign as independent reading *Adam of the Road,* the last half of chapter 22, "Adam Helps a Plowman."

Grades 7–9: Read together or assign as independent reading *The Prince and the Pauper,* chapter 33, "Edward as King."

Book of Centuries Timeline

John Calvin writes "Institutes of the Christian Religion," defining Protestant beliefs (1509–1564)

Grades 10–12: Read together or assign as independent reading *Famous Men of the Renaissance and Reformation,* chapter 28, "John Calvin," and ask for a written narration.

Lesson 173: Visit 35 to the Caribbean & 2 Corinthians 12 and 13

Materials Needed

- *Visits to South & Central America and Australia*
- Bible
- 2 Corinthians envelope with Courage paper
- *Life in the Word* (grades 7–12)

Family Geography: Complete visit 35 in *Visits to South & Central America and Australia.*

Family Bible Study: Display the 2 Corinthians envelope and Courage paper and ask students what they recall about this epistle so far. Explain that in today's reading Paul finished listing his qualifications as an apostle of Jesus Christ and urged any unrepentant Corinthians to repent before he arrived.

Read together 2 Corinthians 12 and 13 (or divide it into smaller portions over several days: 12:1–10, 12:11–21, 13:1–14). Encourage students to listen for circumstances or actions that would involve courage.

Focus on 2 Corinthians 12:8–10. Discuss: Why didn't God take away the physical problem that was troubling Paul when Paul asked Him to? How does Christ's power shine more brightly in our weaknesses? Does it require courage to live with a physical problem? Where can a person find such courage?

Ask students to summarize the main ideas of today's passage. Discuss how those ideas might involve courage. Record students' findings on the Courage paper and return it to the envelope.

Grades 7–12: Help students to complete or assign as independent work *Life in the Word,* chapter 11, "Character Study on Titus," lesson 2.

Lesson 174: One Thousand Years of History

Materials Needed

- *A Castle with Many Rooms: The Story of the Middle Ages*
- *The Stuff They Left Behind: From the Days of the Middle Ages*
- *The Prince and the Pauper* (grades 7–9)
- *Voices of the Renaissance and Reformation* (grades 10–12)

Family: Display and discuss the picture of Florence Cathedral in *The Stuff They Left Behind: From the Days of the Middle Ages.* Ask students what they recall from previous chapters about the changes that moved the world out of the Middle Ages. Look again at the map of Europe in the 15th Century, page 283 in *A Castle with Many Rooms,* to prompt narration and discussion. Read together *A Castle with Many Rooms: The Story of the Middle Ages,* chapter 32, "One Thousand Years of History."

Grades 7–9: Read together or assign as independent reading *The Prince and the Pauper,* Conclusion.

Grades 10–12: Assign Calvin's preface to his Commentary Upon the Psalms, the Geneva Confession, and any other Calvin excerpts of your choice in *Voices of the Renaissance and Reformation,* pages 161–182.

Book of Centuries Timeline

Lesson 175: Various History Readings

Materials Needed

- *Adam of the Road* (grades 4–6)
- *The Prince and the Pauper,* if needed (grades 7–9)
- *Famous Men of the Renaissance and Reformation* (grades 10–12)
- *Voices of the Renaissance and Reformation* (grades 10–12)

Grades 1–3: Use today to finish any reading from this term as needed.

Grades 4–6: Read together or assign as independent reading *Adam of the Road,* chapter 23, "Loud Sing Cuckoo!"

Grades 7–9: Use today to catch up and finish reading *The Prince and the Pauper* if needed.

Grades 10–12: Read together or assign as independent reading *Famous Men of the Renaissance and Reformation,* chapter 29, "John Knox," and ask for a written narration. Also assign his "History of the Reformation of Scotland" in *Voices of the Renaissance and Reformation,* pages 183–187.

John Knox carries the Reformation to Scotland (1514–1572)

Tip: *Make sure older children are up to date with their* Discovering Doctrine *notebooks and their Book of Centuries entries.*

Lesson 176: History Catch Up, Exam, or Project

Materials Needed

- (optional) Materials for hands-on project

Family: Use today to catch up on any history reading you need to finish, or use the questions below for the students' exam on Middle Ages history studied so far. You may also use the history lessons this week to do an optional hands-on project if you would prefer.

Grades 1–3: Tell about how books used to be made by hand and how

Book of Centuries Timeline

Gutenberg changed that process.
Grades 4–6: Describe what life was like for a minstrel in the Middle Ages.
Grades 7–9: Compare and contrast life in the Middle Ages as a prince and as a pauper. What part of the story stood out to you most?
Grades 10–12: Tell all you know about Leonardo da Vinci, including his various works, his notebooks, his research, and his personal characteristics.

Optional Hands-On Project: Select a hands-on project from the Links and Tips page at http://simplycm.com/middle-ages-links.

Lesson 177: History Catch Up, Exam, or Project

Materials Needed

- (optional) Materials for hands-on project

Family: Use today to catch up on any history reading you need to finish, or use the questions below for the students' exam on Middle Ages history studied so far. You may also do an optional hands-on project.
Grades 1–3: Tell what it was like to live in a castle.
Grades 4–6: Explain Gutenberg's idea for a printing press.
Grades 7–9: Write one week's worth of diary entries for either Johannes Gutenberg or Martin Luther.
Grades 10–12: Tell all you know about the sea explorers of this era, including (a) Christopher Columbus, (b) Vasco da Gama, (c) Amerigo Vespucci, (d) Vasco Nunez de Balboa, (e) Ferdinand Magellan. What were their discoveries and what did they contribute to those who followed after them?

Optional Hands-On Project: Continue your selected hands-on project or start a new one if desired.

Lesson 178: Visit 36 to the Caribbean & Bible Exam

Materials Needed

- *Visits to South & Central America and Australia*

Family Geography: Complete visit 36 in *Visits to South & Central America and Australia.*

Family Bible Exam: Use today to catch up on any Bible reading you need to finish, or use the questions below for the students' exam on the epistles they have studied.
Family: Tell what you know about the two epistles to the Corinthians that you have studied. And/or tell about the writer, recipients, and main theme

of each epistle you studied this year: James; Galatians; 1, 2 Thessalonians; 1, 2 Corinthians.

Book of Centuries Timeline

Tip: *It is up to you whether to ask your students to do one or both narration prompts given.*

Grades 7–12: Write (a) a summary of your findings for the topical study on weakness and (b) a description of your findings for the character study on Titus. What did you study and what did you learn?

Lesson 179: History Catch Up, Exam, or Project

Materials Needed

- (optional) Materials for hands-on project

Family: Use today to catch up on any history reading you need to finish, or use the questions below for the students' exam on Middle Ages history studied so far. You may also do an optional hands-on project.
Grades 1–3: Tell the story of William Tyndale, the Bible smuggler.
Grades 4–6: Tell all you know about Martin Luther and the Reformation.
Grades 7–9: Explain what each of these terms stands for and how each one factored into sweeping changes across the world: (a) Renaissance, (b) Reformation.
Grades 10–12: Describe how not all men who separated from the Roman church were worthy to follow. Give at least two examples of false teachers who arose during the Reformation.

Optional Hands-On Project: Continue your selected hands-on project or start a new one if desired.

Lesson 180: History Catch Up, Exam, or Project

Materials Needed

- (optional) Materials for hands-on project

Family: Use today to catch up on any history reading you need to finish, or use the questions below for the students' exam on Middle Ages history studied so far. You may also do an optional hands-on project.
Grades 1–3: Tell your favorite story from the Middle Ages.
Grades 4–6: Explain Copernicus' belief about the heavens.
Grades 7–9: Explain what each of these terms stands for and how each one factored into more sweeping changes across the world: (a) Exploration, (b) Scientific Revolution.

Book of Centuries Timeline

Grades 10–12: The author of *Famous Men of the Renaissance and Reformation* states, "Their lives also show us that secular government more often gets it wrong than right when it meddles in the affairs of the church." Prove or disprove this statement, citing specific examples from the lives of the men of the Reformation.

Optional Hands-On Project: Finish your selected hands-on project.

Helpful Information

Why I Wrote These Lessons

I love to teach Bible history along with world events, and the first three lesson plan books in this series focus on Bible history from Genesis through Acts. Some time is spent studying world events that happened during those years, but the emphasis is on Biblical history.

With this fourth lesson plan book, the focus changes a little. We no longer have Biblical events to study, and world history picks up the pace. So with this fourth book, we delve into learning about people who lived in the past since the time of the book of Acts, and we combine that study with timeless truths from the epistles.

The lessons in this book will walk you through living books to read, Scripture passages to study, and map activities to do. You'll also find narration ideas, teaching tips, exam questions, and Book of Centuries dates.

One of my main goals is to show you how you can teach the same historical time period to all of your children at the same time, no matter what grades they are in. I firmly believe in the advantages that a one-room schoolhouse approach can bring. You will save time in both planning and teaching, and your children will grow together in community as they learn together and help each other.

Please keep in mind that this study is just a collection of suggestions. I'm simply passing along these suggestions to, hopefully, save you some time and give you some ideas. You know your children much better than I do, so feel free to change, add, or omit as you see fit. Remember, I used the books that were available to me; they may not be available to you. Don't be afraid to substitute.

Most of all, encourage the older children to help the younger, and allow the younger to look over the shoulder of the older; and together, enjoy these studies of history, geography, and God's Word.

Charlotte Mason Methods Used in This Study

Living Books

Probably the most well known of Charlotte Mason's methods is her use of living books instead of dry, factual textbooks. Living books are usually written by one person who has a passion for the subject and writes in conversational or narrative style. The books pull you into the subject and involve your emotions, so it's easy to remember the events and facts. Living books make the subject "come alive." The books used in this study are living books. If you make a substitution, please do your best to select a living book.

Bible Readings: The Bible is the best living book! And Charlotte encouraged us to give our children plenty of direct contact with the Bible itself, not feed them just watered down retellings. So you will find throughout the lessons, the Scripture passages to read aloud directly from the Bible.

Narration

When you ask a child to narrate, you're asking him to tell back in his own words what he just saw, heard, or read. The narration can be oral or written or drawn—whatever. Because the child must think through the information and determine how to present it, mixed with his own opinion and impressions, this method of evaluation requires a much higher thinking level than mere fill-in-the-blank or answer-the-posed-question-with-a-fact methods. When requesting a child to narrate, word the question in an open, essay-type form, such as "Tell all you know about ___" or "Describe ___."

Oral Narration with Many Children: Usually it's good to start with the youngest child, then work your way up the ages asking if each has anything to add. However, if you use this approach every single time, the older ones might get complacent. ("No, nothing to add.") So you can mix things up a little by calling on any child at random to start the narration sometimes. Not knowing who will be selected to give the oral narration keeps everybody alert and listening. The key is to have one child start the narration and then have the others add to it, not repeat it. That mental exercise of remembering what was already mentioned and searching through your mind for something new to talk about is also a plus!

Written Narration: Older children can be expected to take the next step and write their narrations. If your older child is not used to doing narration, give him several weeks or months to get used to the idea and have some practice narrating orally first. It's harder to keep your train of thought when you have to also think about the mechanics of writing, punctuating, capitalizing, and all such trappings, so make sure your child is adept and successful with organizing and expressing his thoughts orally before adding the writing aspect. Once he is an "old pro" at oral narrations, you can ease him into the written narrations by requiring just one a week or so to begin with. The lessons in this book will give suggestions for some written narrations. You can determine which of your students can handle those assignments.

Also keep in mind that you can do narration in many ways. Oral is the quickest and simplest. But if you would like to keep things fresh, you can have the children express what they learned in various ways. We have a list of narration ideas on our website that might help you: http://simplycm.com/narration-ideas.

Book of Centuries

A Book of Centuries is like a timeline in a notebook. As its name suggests, each two-page spread in the book is devoted to one hundred years—a century—of history. Each student creates his or her own book, recording historical events and names of importance, along with pictures, poems, quotes, and anything else that makes the book individual. You can also add written narrations, illustrations from the Internet, or titles of books you've read that are set in that time period. As they add more history to the book, the students begin to make relations between people who lived in the same era.

Books of Centuries can be as simple or elaborate as you desire. If you want a simple one, download a free Book of Centuries template at http://simplycm.com/BOC.

We recommend each student in grades 7–12 create his own Book of Centuries. If your students are not yet old enough to take on the responsibility of their own Books of Centuries, you could create one together as a family.

Watch for helpful dates in the timeline column throughout the lessons in this book. You don't have to add every event listed; feel free to pick and choose. (Note: A "c" beside a date stands for "circa," which means "about" or "approximately.")

Suggestions toward Calculating Credits

Keeping track of high school credits is always a challenge but not that hard once you get the hang of it. You can calculate the credits based on actual time spent interacting with the material, or you can calculate credits based on the amount of work involved. Most authorities agree that if you are calculating based on actual time spent, a credit is awarded for every 120–180 hours spent on task, with 150 being average.

For the completion of grades 7–9 or 10–12 assignments in this *Middle Ages, Renaissance, Reformation and Epistles* study, **I suggest that students should be awarded 1 credit for World History/Geography, plus 1⁄3 credit for Bible.** Usually Geography is included with History and considered one course of study.

Below are details demonstrating how the credit suggestions for this study were calculated. The calculations for Hours Spent are an estimated average. The calculations below for the Course Work Detail assume the student completed all of the readings and assignments given in these lesson plans for grades 7–9 or 10–12.

Hours Spent

History & Geography—1 Credit
Average 4.5 hours per week x 36 weeks = 162 hours

Bible—1⁄3 Credit
Average 1.25 hours per week x 36 weeks = 45 hours

Course Work Detail

History

Grades 7–9
1984 pages read in 11 books
16 written narrations
16 artifacts studied
Book of Centuries project
3 essay exams

Grades 10–12
2336 pages read in 13 books
65 written narrations
16 artifacts studied
Book of Centuries project
3 essay exams

Geography

Grades 7–12
26 map studies and drills
308 pages read in 3 books
37 historical map work lessons

Bible

Grades 7–12
6 New Testament epistles read
103-page Bible study completed
Discovering Doctrine project
3 essay exams